Let No One Despise You

Let No One Despise You

Emerging Christians in a Post-Christian Society

Tony Beard

WIPF & STOCK · Eugene, Oregon

LET NO ONE DESPISE YOU
Emerging Christians in a Post-Christian Society

Copyright © 2020 Tony Beard. All rights reserved. Except for brief quotations in critical publications or reviews, no part of this book may be reproduced in any manner without prior written permission from the publisher. Write: Permissions, Wipf and Stock Publishers, 199 W. 8th Ave., Suite 3, Eugene, OR 97401.

Wipf & Stock
An Imprint of Wipf and Stock Publishers
199 W. 8th Ave., Suite 3
Eugene, OR 97401

www.wipfandstock.com

PAPERBACK ISBN: 978-1-7252-6202-7
HARDCOVER ISBN: 978-1-7252-6199-0
EBOOK ISBN: 978-1-7252-6200-3

Manufactured in the U.S.A. 05/07/20

Unless otherwise indicated, biblical quotations are taken from The Holy Bible, English Standard Version® (ESV®), copyright © 2001 by Crossway, a publishing ministry of Good News Publishers. All rights reserved.

Contents

Preface	*vii*
Acknowledgments	*xi*

PART 1: LET NO ONE DESPISE YOU — 1

1. Timothy	3
2. Emerging Adulthood	11
3. Young Adults Matter	19
4. Spirit of Immediacy	30
5. A Brief Word of Caution	39

PART 2: YOU WILL BE HATED — 43

6. Whatever Happened to Timothy?	45
7. What Is Persecution?	54
8. Pre-Persecution in the West	60
9. Persecution Around the World	73
10. Persecution from False Teaching	83
11. But There Is Hope	95

PART 3: LOVE THEM ANYWAY — 101

12. Love Is a Verb	103
13. Love God	107
14. Love Others	114
15. Sharing the Gospel	126

Conclusion	*132*
Bibliography	*135*

Preface

One of my best friends (and former college roommate) and his wife were leading a young adult group at their church when they asked me to speak at their annual winter retreat held in upstate Pennsylvania. I was humbled by this invitation. They trusted me to deliver a message to emerging adult Christians in their care for discipleship. This wasn't something to take lightly!

They asked me because I had been working with college students for years, led college student and young adult Bible studies, and was in the loop with the issues Christians faced, particularly young Christians, in the public sphere. I never claimed to be an expert, but I was confident I could share some important thoughts with these young adults, ranging from upper high school to post-college (and a number who were out of high school, but never attended college).

This is an age group I feel very connected with and have a deep desire to discuss faith with. My own greatest development in faith occurred over the four years I attended college. My greatest period of "backsliding" was in the several years that followed college, as I was simply lost without my college community. For four years in college I regularly attended fellowship nights, led Bible studies, prayed with friends, and attended retreats. The next three years I was in a career that was a terrible fit, had no home church, relied too heavily on podcasts for spiritual growth, and dated a nice girl I should never have dated. I know I am not the only one who has faced these challenges.

It has never been easy leaving high school to head to college, enlist in the military, or enter the workforce. But now? Now it's even crazier with trials previous generations never faced. For any young person this is a challenge. Where are you going to college? What are you studying? What job is that going to lead to? You're not going to college? Why not?

Preface

Couldn't you get in? Those questions are just the start of it, and each person you meet over the course of the first year out of high school asks them. Once you're out of college or have been working a few years it turns into: When are you getting married? When are you having kids? Isn't it time you settled down? It's about as predictable as the sun rising or my four-year-old daughter asking "Why?"

For the *Christian* young person it becomes even more complicated. As followers of Christ we are called to a lifestyle not often depicted (at least not accurately) in the latest *National Lampoon's* movie about college. Sex, booze, and weed are just the beginning of easy temptations, seemingly existing as rites of passage at the typical American college or university. This doesn't even include the pressures of academic faithfulness or attacks on Christian theology or truth in general. While most philosophy classes don't resemble the one from *God's Not Dead*, there is more often than not an indifference towards Christianity at best, and a low-level hostility at worst.

In his highly influential 2011 book *Lost in Transition*, Notre Dame sociology professor Christian Smith explained:

> Studies agree that the transition to adulthood today is more complex, disjointed, and confusing than it was in past decades. The steps through schooling, a first real job, marriage, and parenthood are simply less well organized and coherent today than they were in the past. At the same time, these years are marked by a historically unparalleled freedom to roam, experiment, learn, move on, and try again.[1]

"Unparalleled freedom" is not a bad thing, but emerging adults, often understood as those in their late teens to late twenties, have largely been inadequately prepared to encounter a world beyond their teenage years. They are arriving at college, entering the military, and going to work unaware of their potential impact for the kingdom of God and unaware of a world very different than what their adolescent years knew. Being a young adult has never been easy, but for Christians in their late teens and twenties today, multiple factors have resulted in generational struggle with identity and purpose. The age of Christendom has faded, and there are less societal expectations on young adults to call themselves Christians. Today's youth have remarkable access to instant gratification, yet report startlingly high levels of stress. The gospel is readily available through technological advances, but emerging adults keep leaving the church.

---

1. Smith et al., *Lost in Transition*, 15

Preface

Young adults may no longer have social or civic expectations to follow Christ, but the gospel is as relevant and vital today as it was fifty or two thousand years ago.

The church needs to raise up the next generation of Christian leaders by encouraging them and preparing them *to be* leaders. Young adults today are capable of such leadership and ministry, yet they are being failed by a society and a church that is lowering the expectations of its youth.

The culture has shifted tremendously in just the last ten to twenty years, and the church was not prepared to make a counterargument to the young adults watching it all unfold. That can no longer be the case, and *Let No One Despise You* helps fill that gap, speaking directly to young adults and ministry leaders alike.

What follows is an adaptation of the talk I gave at that young adult retreat a few years ago. The scope is simple:

1. Youth is not an obstacle to Christ.
2. The world is an enemy of God.
3. The best way to live in the world is to love.

Those ideas make up this book's three sections.

Is this book for young Christians or for those who work with young Christians? Both. My intention is to speak directly to young adults through this book, but hopefully it can be fruitful for those ministering to this age group as well.

I hope my words positively impact at least a few young people. The format of the book is encouragement, a dose of reality, and more encouragement. May our eyes always be open to the disappointment of the world, and may our hearts always be filled with the hope of Holy Spirit and long for the kingdom to come.

Acknowledgments

I wish to thank all the many young adults who have allowed me to be part of their faith walk over the past however many years. I also wish to thank all the many servants investing their time in college and young adult ministries. I know my faith has been shaped by countless individuals who invested in my own emerging adulthood years.

Many of these experiences and life stories would not have been possible without Justin Risser and Jordan Martin. Together we have traveled our walks with Christ side by side since the first weeks of college. My brother William Verdon has had to put up with me even longer than those two, and he was the first person to take the time to read an early draft of this manuscript.

It's remarkable how God has consistently put others in my life when I've needed them, which includes Patrick Anderson, a part of my later emerging adulthood years. Also incredibly influential during those years was Pastor Eric Miller. More recently, God has been using Ryan Bechtold and Tory Allison in my life as well.

My first real conversation about the publishing industry was with Byron Borger at his bookstore, Hearts and Minds. I'm also grateful for Dan Sheard's helpful insight on thesis cohesion (although I'm still not sure it's there!) and encouragement of the project.

Of course, thank you to my parents, Jim and Carol Beard, for encouraging me in my passions, be it baseball or writing.

No book would have been written without my loving wife, Angela Beard. Angela believes I can do the things I only dream of doing. Her faith in me, as well as her life partnership, go beyond anything I deserve. Also, thanks for taking care of Priscilla and Bo while I went off to the coffee shop to write! I would have never seen this project through without her encouragement.

Acknowledgments

Thank you to everyone at Wipf and Stock who had a hand in bringing this project to completion.

Finally, thank you Lord for whatever use you have placed in me to fulfill your purposes.

Part 1

Let No One Despise You

1

Timothy

Age may only be a number, but it's often the most important one. Travel most of the United States and ask someone who is 15 if there is any difference between 15 and 16 as they stare off longingly at the used car lot. Being 17 years and 364 days old makes you a juvenile, but add one more day and you magically convert into a legal adult. Folks line up at the bars just before midnight of their 21st birthday to legally enter and drink. And for some completely random reason, you need to be 25 to rent a car. I have no idea why.

So, sure, age is just a number, but that number has relevance and we infer a lot about someone based on that number. Parents have seemingly arbitrary rules like, "No dating until you're 15." Now, that's probably not a bad rule, but we have all met really smart and responsible 14-year-olds and really dense 16-year-olds. Being alive for 15 years does not supernaturally prepare you for the dating world.

Sometimes this age number prevents young adults from doing what they passionately want to do, perhaps like taking on leadership roles in church. And, unfortunately, when someone younger takes on roles some believe they are not yet ready for, jealousy and bitterness may arise. But what about being despised? Is anyone ever really despised just because someone young takes on major responsibilities?

"Despise" may be a strong word for what most experience, but "dismissive" sure fits the bill. Many young adult Christians are leaving attractional and entertainment-based youth ministries focused on fun, food, and fellowship, with faith popping up only on occasion. How often are youth groups creating a lasting difference or learning how to engage in anything outside of their church bubble? Sit here, be entertained, bring your friends next week, but don't ask too many questions!

Even if a youth group gathering is more than Sunday or Wednesday night busywork, how many are being trained to lead the church? A dismissive attitude towards the role of teenagers in the church results in ill-prepared young adult Christians. Young adults are not prepared to be leaders by being told as teens they are not leaders. They are prepared to be leaders by being told they are not leaders *yet*, and given meaningful and appropriate responsibilities to learn how to lead. Ideally, this is done hand in hand with mentors.

Having a mentor who looks out for one's best interests and engages in honest conversations about what responsibilities the mentee is capable of is critical, especially for young adults. While this may result in the mentor agreeing that the mentee is not ready for a new challenge, a good mentor helps sketch out ways for the person to *become* ready. This could include drafting out short—and long-term goals, creating a roadmap on how to get there, and being available for support, questions, prayer, and dialogue along the way.

During the early church period the Apostle Paul mentored Timothy, and addressed this concern of how to approach those who did not think he was capable of serving Christ in a leadership role beyond his years. Paul believed Timothy was ready and was prepared to serve God despite a younger age, writing to Timothy:

> Command and teach these things. Let no one despise you for your youth, but set the believers an example in speech, in conduct, in love, in faith, in purity. Until I come, devote yourself to the public reading of Scripture, to exhortation, to teaching. Do not neglect the gift you have, which was given you by prophecy when the council of elders laid their hands on you. Practice these things, immerse yourself in them, so that all may see your progress. Keep a close watch on yourself and on the teaching. Persist in this, for by doing so you will save both yourself and your hearers. (1 Tim 4:11–16)

Young Christians ought to be encouraged: Let no one despise you for your youth. The word of God commands that you are not to be scorned simply for living too few years on earth. Being grafted into the community of Christ sets you on the course of sanctification, that is, the path of becoming holy and more like Jesus. Sanctification is a process. Some may be further along in this process than you, but it is still the same process. One's age *can* affect this development, but there is no direct correlation. We all come to know Christ at different ages, and some of us have different churches and support around us that can impact our progress. Additionally, some of us just process new ideas and information more quickly than others. If you are in Christ, your salvation and call to serve and glorify God are no different whether you are 20 years old or 80 years old. I think this is what was behind Paul's words of encouragement to Timothy.

Who was Timothy?

Timothy is first introduced to the reader in Acts 16. Paul meets Timothy in Lystra, which was a city in the Roman province of Galatia (modern day Turkey). We learn Timothy's father was a Greek and his mother a Jew. This placed Timothy is a unique position: because of his father, he had access to the civil and educational opportunities expected of a Greek, but because of his mother, also the religious teachings of the Jews. Consider it similar to dual citizenship, and having the rights afforded by two different nations. Luke, the writer of the book of Acts, adds that Timothy was "well spoken of by the brothers at Lystra" (Acts 16:2). That is, other Christians in that region are saying good things about him.

These passages from 1 Timothy 4 and Acts 16 permit us to reasonably assume: 1) Timothy was considered a youth in his society, and 2) he was active enough in the early Christian church that some people Paul cared about in Lystra thought highly of Timothy. These two descriptions could very well be you. Perhaps you are the high school student helping lead worship a couple Sundays a month, or the college student away from home, volunteering with the local church's youth group. Maybe you went straight into the workforce, but are sure to stop by men's Bible study at 6:30 a.m. before you head off to your job. Timothy was the young person some of the elders in the church took notice of, as did Paul.

Much of Paul's ministry occurred while traveling or even under arrest. This means he could not always be physically present with all the churches he helped establish. Studying his three missionary journeys in Acts shows us he was preaching the gospel in as many places as he could. His letters to churches gave imperative instruction, but whom would he write to? Who would represent Paul? Who could he trust in the various cities while he was away? Paul partnered with many individuals to further the kingdom of God, including Timothy, Barnabas, Titus, Lydia, Aquila, and Priscilla.

Part 1: Let No One Despise You

Each of these men and women of faith played important roles in laying the foundation of Christianity after Jesus' resurrection, but in Scripture Timothy has been given special attention. He ministered in a number of cities, including Corinth, Ephesus, and Thessalonica.

In 1 Timothy 4 Paul not only tells Timothy to not let anyone get on his case about being young, but Paul also encourages him. Paul gives Timothy instructions to demonstrate that despite his youth, he is a leader in the body of Christ. In this passages he advises Timothy to do five things: set an example to other Christians, read Scripture in public, exhort, teach, and not neglect the gifts given to him.

Concerning the first instruction of setting an example, have you ever been told by a parent, a teacher, or perhaps a pastor that you are to set an example for someone younger? If you're an older brother or sister, you have probably heard it a million times. I'll admit it's my go-to when my four-year-old is misbehaving around her younger brother! For others, maybe a parent at church thanked you for spending time with their child who is several years younger than you: "Thank you for setting such a great example for my daughter." The funny thing here is that Timothy, *the one who is portrayed as younger than many in the community around him*, is to set the example. This seems entirely backwards.

We too often assume that with age automatically comes wisdom. And while age very often does bring wisdom, it is not an immutable law of nature. As Voddie Baucham has said, "Maturity in Christians is marked not by gray hair, but by the fruit believers bear in keeping with their sanctification."[1]

Surely we can all think of folks much older than us who have been unable to keep a job because of laziness, or are spendthrift, or despite attending church for decades still looks suspiciously towards someone with a different shade of skin. Again, this is because age does not automatically bring wisdom, rather, "the Lord gives wisdom; from his mouth comes knowledge and understanding" (Prov 2:6). So if you want to be wise and set a great example, it's not a matter of living longer than others, but a deep understanding of the word of God. And while an advanced age provides opportunity for an individual to know God better due to more time spent alive, not everyone has taken advantage of that time.

Please understand what I am saying and what I am not saying. I *am* saying age does not automatically produce wisdom. I *am not* saying to assume the older Christians in your life are not wise. They most likely have a

---

1. Baucham, *Family Shepherds*, 30.

wealth of wisdom ready to bequeath upon you. But the young adult is not absent of any of his or her own wisdom.

Paul also writes to Timothy to publicly read Scripture. Have you ever been asked to read Scripture at your church service? This is less common at more modern churches, but used to be a typical part of a church's liturgy. However, many older denominations still practice more traditional church service components, such as the reading of Scripture.

When I first started going to church as a teenager, I attended a United Methodist church. The service would include scriptural readings from both the Old and New Testaments that did not necessarily correlate with the sermon. These readings were done by pretty much anyone the pastor trusted. I never read in front of the church, probably for good reason (that reason being a crushing fear of public speaking). Speaking the Word of God in public ought to be a task regarded very reverently, and Paul instructed the young Timothy to do it.

In addition to reading Scripture in public, Timothy was charged with exhortation. To exhort basically means to tell people what to do (although there may be a more polite way of saying that). Timothy was not only given permission to exhort, but was ordered to give instruction to the local church. He was able to tell others what's up. Given that we know Timothy was young, at least in comparison to those around him, this might come as a surprise. The thing is, though, God has demonstrated time and again he will raise up whom he wants as leaders. Whether God picks a stutterer to command Pharaoh to release the Jews, calls a guy hiding from his enemies a "mighty man of valor," or chooses the shepherd runt of a large family as the king of Israel, God demands faithfulness, not eloquence, strength, size, or even age. Our God is Lord over everything. He does not need any skill or talent a human possesses to accomplish his will; one's faithfulness will suffice.

Timothy's fourth instruction was to teach. Even today this seems like a bold directive. Probably the most common teachers in our lives are our high school teachers, our college professors, or our church pastors. With a few exceptions, they have all probably received some sort of formal education or certification to validate their credentials to teach. States have various certification processes for teachers, and different Christian denominations have seminaries and ordinations for their pastors. This means an agency tests and then verifies someone's competency in a given area and confirms they are qualified to teach others. That isn't the case

Part 1: Let No One Despise You

here. Timothy would have received his education from Paul, who is now trusting him enough to teach others.

I am sure you have had some young and cool teacher at one point or another during your middle school or high school years, even if only a student teacher. Before I decided to work in higher education, I taught English for several years and assumed I was that young and cool teacher who could connect to my students. As it turned out, I was a really bad teacher. It didn't matter if I was young or cool (which I probably wasn't), because I did not know how to teach. At this time I was not very successful at taking a subject and converting it into knowledge for a classroom full of students, and if I couldn't do that, what was the point of teaching? Timothy was that young and popular Christian in town, but he also actually knew what he was talking about.

You might not have Paul sitting with you and answering your questions to prepare you to teach others, but you do have Scripture. And plenty of resources like commentaries and books on theology. And, hopefully, a pastor and/or Christian mentor speaking into your life and leading you. Seminaries are great if that is what you are called to, but they are not required for a life of faithful living and teaching in many capacities. If you are willing to learn, you can teach others.

Finally, Timothy was directed not to neglect his gift. Paul saw something in Timothy, regardless of his age. He knew God was doing something special through Timothy and encouraged him not to ignore that. The same can probably be said of you. I have no idea what gifts God has given you, but my prayer is you that have someone around to help identify them.

Now, I am going to be blunt: the gift you have might not be the one you want. I wanted to be a worship leader, but I can't sing or play any instruments (nor do I have the discipline to learn). So that did not really work out for me. Yet it became clear later on that I am gifted with counseling skills, and this has led me to opportunities to mentor and disciple young adults. Although I wanted to be front and center strumming on guitar belting out "Awesome God" (Gen-Zers: this was a really popular worship song in the 1990s), I have been drawn closer to God through the use of the talents he did bless me with.

Gifts (not limiting to just "spiritual gifts") could include hospitality, listening to others, prayer, artistry, public speaking, carpentry, kindness, and so on and so on. The point is not that you get one gift and then you find a job corresponding with it. The point is God has given you talents, even

Timothy

if you do not think they are such, and you ought to find ways to glorify him with those gifts. Some may use those gifts in a profession and receive compensation for it. Many others will use those talents in various non-professional ministry. If that sounds like a bummer, keep in mind Jesus was never paid for his healings, teachings, and dying on the cross. Utilizing your gifts is not about a paycheck, but about glorifying God.

First Timothy 4:11–16 is a pretty obvious place to start when discussing the challenges of being young and being Christian. Chances are you have had a youth pastor teach on this some Sunday morning or Wednesday evening.

What Is Youth?

If you are reading this book, you're probably young, or you work with young people. I am a big believer that when we discuss topics we need to define the terms we use. So what do we mean when we use the word "youth"?

Taking the easiest route, here is the *Dictionary.com* definition: "The period between childhood and adult age."[2]

Wow, okay. Not super helpful, Internet dictionary. Kind of vague, no?

Still, its vagueness can help prove a point: youth cannot be defined by a specific age. Rather, youth is an amorphous stage that exists somewhere between playing t-ball and collecting Social Security. Pablo Picasso (allegedly) said that "Youth has no age." Crazy portraits aside, he is onto something. Youth is not about how many years you have lived on earth because it is too relative for that.

Consider your parents. You probably think they are somewhat old. Yet your grandparents probably think your parents are somewhat young. This is perspective. Think of when you moved from elementary school to middle school. Somehow, despite being a year older, you actually became among the youngest in the school. Perspective.

Or think of it this way. Let's say your favorite football player is 32 years old. Is that young or old? A 2012 study found that a group of running backs "peaked at age 26, and had a four-year prime from ages 24 to 27 . . . Several running backs weren't even active in the league by the time they were 30. Among all running backs . . . there was a very steady decline from age 26 to age 31 and then a sharper decline at age 32." On top of that, most were

2. "Youth."

Part 1: Let No One Despise You

"essentially done by age 34." So if your favorite player is a 32-year-old running back, yes, he's old.[3]

However, in 2012 over half of the NFL had kickers above the age of 30.[4] So if your favorite player is a 32-year-old kicker: 1) no he's not old, and 2) are you related to him, because why else would a kicker be your favorite player?

So youth is relative. Think about who you spend your time around. In some circles (perhaps family) you are the youngest. In other circles (perhaps youth group or work) you might be among the oldest. Ultimately, the point here is that we cannot nail down a perfect understanding of who is and who is not young.

Which brings us back to 1 Timothy 4:11–16. In these verses, the Greek word translated as "youth" is *neotes*. Think of other words like neophyte (a beginner) or neonatal (something relating to a newborn child). Both these words indicate something new or something young.

However, here is information that might revolutionize how you read this verse: *neotes* could be used to describe someone *up to the age of 40*. In all likelihood, with the evidence we have, Timothy was probably somewhere in his 30s when Paul wrote this letter to him. This may seem surprising. In our Western society we don't usually think of someone in their 30s as young (although this information pleases the thirty-something writer of this book).

Nevertheless, knowing the idea of youth is open to interpretation, Paul's words are still vitally relevant to young adults today, even defined as being 18 to 29. Again, youth is relative and we need to deconstruct our concepts of the term. We cannot just say someone who is 18 is young and someone who is 29 is not because there are too many factors, circumstances, and, yes, perspectives to be that concrete. We can't necessarily say the 18 year-old is not capable of helping lead a ministry while the 19-year-old is. Think of who is considered young in our society and in different circles: the freshman girl on your soccer team, your new coworker at the office, the just-married couple in your home group. Depending on where we are, we might be the youngest or we might be the oldest. Take down some barriers of who you think is young and who isn't. Like Picasso said, "youth has no age."

---

3. Stuart, "Closer Look."
4. Baldwin, "NFL Kickers' Careers."

2

Emerging Adulthood

My wife and I used to be really into *New Girl*. The first couple of seasons were hilarious! The series revolved around several characters in their 20s rooming together in a Los Angeles loft. The content was a little coarse, and ultimately contributed to our eventual disinterest. The other major factor was the repetition. Some of the characters just didn't grow up or mature, which was actually part of the joke. Still, when you are a newly married 20-something paying off college loans, saving up for a house, and planning on a family, watching characters doing the same thing today they did five years ago just becomes boring. Stunted personal growth may make a successful comedy, but it is a recipe for a disastrous spiritual life.

Unfortunately, this is the message many Christian young adults receive about growing up: *Don't do it!* It's entirely true individuals will mature at their own rate, but glorifying a lack of maturity and encouraging youthful indiscretion is not helping anyone. While youth is a tenuous idea, the truth is, you should not want to stay young forever.

The American media sells this idea that staying young is the dream, and that to be young means acting irrational, emotional, and reckless. Music, TV, blogs—many of them will tell you to stay young for as long as you can. I am telling you that as Christians, we need to reject this idea. It's especially important for churches to recognize they are doing themselves a disservice by not better preparing their teens and young adults for our post-Christian society.

In 2000 an article titled "Emerging Adulthood" by Jeffrey Arnett was published in *American Psychologist* (it was later published as a full book). The overall theme is not only that individuals take different paths to adulthood,

Part 1: Let No One Despise You

but that a whole new life stage exists that prolongs one's attainment of adulthood. I first learned about this theory while in grad school. Our cohort was a collection of 20-somethings, mostly trying to figure out life and this theory became our mantra. Even then, though, I found it a little disheartening.

Arnett introduces the concept of emerging adulthood by describing it as a proposed "new conception of development for the period from the late teens through the twenties, with a focus on ages 18–25." He continues, saying he intends to "support the idea that emerging adulthood is a distinct period demographically, subjectively, and in terms of identity explorations," but admits that "emerging adulthood *exists only in cultures that allow young people a prolonged period of independent role exploration during the late teens and twenties.*"[1]

Emerging adulthood certainly sounds like an intriguing idea at first. It describes a grey area in between adolescence and adulthood. The issue, however, is that this theory also describes prolonging the period of role exploration. While it takes some longer than others to explore who we are (identity) and what we are made for (purpose), a culture that encourages an open-ended search with no reinforcement on the importance of realization is begging for trouble.

There comes a point when questions need answers. Extending the time period to search may sometimes be required for an individual, but a society that values the exploration over the discovery will quickly lack stability.

Arnett continues his introduction by explaining:

> Emerging adulthood is neither adolescence nor young adulthood but is theoretically and empirically distinct from them both. Emerging adulthood is distinguished by relative independence from social roles and from normative expectations. Having left the dependency of childhood and adolescence, and having not yet entered the enduring responsibilities that are normative in adulthood, emerging adults often explore a variety of possible life directions in love, work, and world views. Emerging adulthood is a time of life when many different directions remain possible, when the scope of independent exploration of life's possibilities is greater for most people than it will be at any other period in the life course.[2]

Emerging adulthood is a theory that does not simply look at the late teens through mid-20s as a *transition time*, but as *its own life stage*. This is

---

1. Arnett, "Emerging Adulthood," 469. Emphasis added.
2. Arnett, "Emerging Adulthood," 469.

difficult to reconcile when we acknowledge that life stages are transitional to begin with. Generally, life stages include infancy, childhood, adolescence, adulthood, and old age. For the young adult, the focus is childhood, adolescence, and adulthood. In many ways, adolescence is very much a transitionary stage that connects childhood to adulthood. However, if we now turn the time transitioning from adolescence to adulthood into its own stage (emerging adulthood), we have now created two additional transitions: the one from adolescence into emerging adulthood and the one from emerging adulthood into adulthood. By treating youth in such a manner, we approvingly extend the time one takes to mature.

Let's use boiling water as an analogy. Boiling water starts with water sitting in a pot (*childhood*). The process ends with boiling water (*adulthood*). Consider the time in between when the water is warming and bubbles start to form as *adolescence*. Emerging adulthood takes that middle stage and segments it further—maybe when a couple of bubbles start reaching the surface of the water or when someone like me says "good enough" and dumps in the pasta anyway. Regardless, emerging adulthood says one transitional period between childhood and adulthood is not good enough, and adds transition into the transition.

Sticking with this analogy, we recognize the time it takes to boil (adolescence) will differ depending on various factors. Was the water placed in the pot frozen or was it already pretty hot? What temperature is the stove set at? Is the stove gas or electric? Is one even using a stove as opposed to cooking over an open fire? Those different factors might ruin the control of the process, but it does not change the three stages: not-boiling water, boiling water, and the time in between. Like water taking longer to boil depending on circumstances, individuals will take longer to pass through adolescence to reach adulthood. Contributing factors could be parenting methods, where one grows up, the quality of the schools attended, learning styles, and many, many more influences. It does not require an additional "emerging adulthood" stage to explain this.

Character Development

Why does any of this matter? Because it has a direct impact on one's character development. Arnett identifies two primary criteria to define the transition into adulthood: "accepting responsibility for one's self and making independent decisions." He continues by stating, "During these years, the character qualities most important to becoming successfully self-sufficient—accepting responsibility for one's self and making independent decisions—are being developed . . . Only after these character qualities have reached fruition and financial independence has been attained do emerging adults experience a subjective change in their developmental status, as they move out of emerging adulthood and into young adulthood."[3]

During this time period of 18 to 25 years old the individual's character is still developing. We can all recognize that character ought to be instilled at a very young age, but we need to acknowledge it is still developing at ages 18 to 25 and older. Maria, who just graduated high school, John, who has been working a minimum wage job since he dropped out of high school five years ago, and Jermaine, who has just received his master's after going straight from high school to college to grad school, are all still developing their character. As Christians, we must develop Christ-like character. Who we are, how we speak, how we think, and how we approach interpersonal and cultural issues must be shaped by Jesus. Our churches and parachurch ministries ought to reflect that. In my own life, I grew more spiritually during my four years of college than I did any other four-year period of my life prior or since. In fact, immediately after college I saw a plateau or even a reversal in my spiritual growth.

See, while in college, I was heavily involved with a chapter of Inter-Varsity Christian Fellowship. There was a group of us who spent inordinate amounts of time around each other. We took classes together, we prayed together, we studied together, we ate together, we led Bible studies together, we cried together, we watched movies together, and we did dumb stuff in Walmart together. And while I openly admit there were plenty of times we should have been better at reaching out to the rest of the college with the message of Christ, we had the fellowship part down.

This fellowship demonstrated mentoring relationships in different forms. IVCF supplied staff workers who were there to support us, and, like every other club on campus, we had advisors from the college staff/faculty to talk to. The upperclassmen mentored (often informally) the younger students. If you were a sophomore, you likely had a senior who was speaking into your life, you had other sophomores to spend time with, and you helped out the freshmen who just arrived. And all of this was relatively easy because life was right there. The staff workers, the advisors, the seniors, the freshmen—*everyone* was right there on or around campus.

---

3. Arnett, "Emerging Adulthood," 473.

When I left college things went awry. That community, as it was, disappeared and I struggled to adjust. My formerly regular and natural fellowship that came Sunday evenings during Bible study, Mondays during intramural softball, Wednesdays during large group InterVarsity meetings, and weekends just hanging out was gone and I felt abandoned. My closest friends were all married within a couple years of graduating college, while I was stuck in neutral without Christian community, involved in a dating relationship I should have never been in, and attending a megachurch where I faded into anonymity. Most my spiritual experiences arrived through podcasts. That is not how one develops character.

Surrounding oneself with a Christian community is especially important during these years. That community helps form one's character. Sociology professor Jonathan P. Hill reports, "Emerging adulthood is a less religious period of life than either childhood or later adulthood."[4] If we are all less inclined to engage our faith during our young adult years, it is that more imperative to stay connected with fellow believers and recognize our roles in society.

Roleless

Part of my own struggle during my emerging adulthood years was not knowing what my role in life was. Talcott Parsons was a sociologist who taught at Harvard for over 45 years. He considered adolescence to be a time of having a "roleless role," but Arnett takes this term and says it "applies much better to emerging adulthood. Emerging adults tend to have a wider scope of possible activities than persons in other age groups because they are less likely to be constrained by role requirements, and this makes their demographic status unpredictable."[5] The argument is that young persons have no role in society, and I think what is being implied is that this is a good thing.

For the Christian, we need to consider this a deceitful concept. Being roleless implies two things: a lack of identity and a lack of purpose. As Christians we should find both our identity and purpose in Christ. Consider the following selections of Scripture on identity:

> So God created man in his own image, in the image of God he created him; male and female he created them. (Gen 1:27)

---

4. Hill, *Emerging Adulthood and Faith*, 63.
5. Arnett, "Emerging Adulthood," 471.

Part 1: Let No One Despise You

> But to all who did receive [Jesus], who believe in his name, he gave the right to become children of God. (John 1:12)

> But you are a chosen race, a royal priesthood, a holy nation, a people for his own possession, that you may proclaim the excellencies of him who called you out of darkness into his marvelous light. Once you were not a people, but now you are God's people; once you had not received mercy, but now you have received mercy. (1 Pet 2:9–10)

And now on purpose:

> He has told you, O man, what is good; and what does the Lord require of you but to do justice, and to love kindness, and to walk humbly with your God? (Mic 6:8)

> "Teacher, which is the great commandment in the Law?" And he said to him, "You shall love the Lord your God with all your heart and with all your soul and with all your mind. This is the great and first commandment. And a second is like it: You shall love your neighbor as yourself. On these two commandments depend all the Law and the Prophets." (Matt 22:36–40)

> Go therefore and make disciples of all nations, baptizing them in the name of the Father and of the Son and of the Holy Spirit, teaching them to observe all that I have commanded you. And behold, I am with you always, to the end of the age." (Matt 28:19–20)

> So, whether you eat or drink, or whatever you do, do all to the glory of God. (1 Cor 10:31)

As Christians, both our *identity* and our *purpose* are to be found in Christ. Yes, this time period of 18 to 25 years old that Arnett has identified will be a time of exploration for the young Christian, just not in the same manner as a non-believer. As followers of Christ, we know where our identity and purpose come from, but it still takes effort to figure out how to express them.

At age 22, Michelle may know she is a child of God and is to love him and love others, but what does that look like in her life? Are her skills in teaching? If so, should she be a school teacher, work her way up to be a school principal or college president, lead Bible studies, or get married and homeschool her children? Maybe Michelle's skills are learning new cultures and connecting with people. Does she become a missionary? If so, does she travel to New Guinea or New Orleans? Long-term or short-term? Does she do urban ministry? Rural?

For the Christian, these natural role explorations need to be seen through the lens of Christ. The highs and lows will come no matter what during this time, but the Christian's ability to navigate this terrain is directly connected to finding one's identity and purpose in Christ. For those of us who work with young Christians, everything we say to them and everything we do with them must point back to Christ. The young Christian may try out a number of jobs, move a bunch of times, and even go out on a lot of dates. As long as all of it is done with the controls firmly in God's hands, that's okay.

Counter to the Gospel

The most critical thing that can be said about a culture which encourages this rolelessness is that it is counter to the gospel message.

The World says: *You do you.*

Christ says: *Deny yourself and follow me.* (Luke 9:23)

The emerging adulthood years may be a time for exploration, but it is not a time to abandon Christ or to pursue selfish ambitions. The church needs to be prepared to minister to this group with understanding and grace. The world today is not what it was when many of our church leaders were in their late teens and twenties.

Compare what many church leaders experienced in their own emerging adulthood years compared to the emerging adulthood years of Generation Z and the younger Millennials. Consider basic differences like transportation and cost of goods, and differences in the job market. What careers today require a college degree, but didn't twenty years ago? Think about all the technological advances. Some leaders may have been in college before PCs were common! Others (like me, possibly the world's oldest Millennial) experienced the bulk of their emerging adulthood years prior to smartphones. Such technology advances allow one to tap a phone a couple times to connect with someone in Ghana. Or to make a needless purchase. Or to download pornography. These are all unique opportunities and temptations that can create cultural misunderstanding between church leaders and emerging adults.

Part 1: Let No One Despise You

For the young Christian, you need to know your identity is in Christ. Jackie Hill Perry wrote, "We are what Christ had done for us; therefore, our ultimate identity is very simple: We are Christians."[6] That is who you are first and foremost. Not a young adult. Not a college dropout. Not a fatherless child. Not a slacker. Not an abuse survivor. Not the sum of any of your successes or failures. Your definitive identity is a child of God.

Similarly, your purpose in in Christ as well. If you think you lack any role in society, you are wrong. Your purpose, or your "calling," is primarily the same as every other Christian: to know God and make him known. We throw the idea of calling around pretty loosely, but Erica Young Reitz makes a great point when she says, "Discerning our calling implies a Caller. If we want to know our calling we need to know our Caller."[7] I take this to mean if we want to discern our purpose in this world, we return immediately to the source of our identity: followers of Christ.

Some define adulthood by things like career, marriage, and home ownership. That may be true. It also might take one longer than others to reach such a status. I know from personal experience. For others, adulthood may simply mean the capability of being responsible for oneself and ability to care for someone in need.

From the time I was in high school, what I wanted most was to be a husband and father. There are three buddies I have who are like brothers, all around the same age as me. One was married at 21, another at 23, and the third at 24. Two of them already had multiple kids running around when I was married at 28 (which is actually about average for an American male, just not in my circle). I know what it is like to feel "left behind" in the Christian community. I get it. Forget that stuff for a moment, because you are not defined by any of it. Your identity is a child of God, a follower of Christ, and residence to the indwelling Holy Spirit. Your purpose is to serve him. Remember those two points and you'll be fine.

---

6. Perry, *Gay Girl, Good God*, 148.
7. Reitz, *After College*, 166.

3

Young Adults Matter

Each social identity that can possibly exist seems to be a niche market for church outreach. Consider what we do for men's ministries and women's ministries. There are men's breakfasts and women's tea parties. Go to a local Christian bookstore and you'll probably find books with titles like *Manly Jesus Slayed Satan and So Can You!: Tips to Being a Mighty Man of Valor* juxtaposed to *Sarah's Secret Source: How to Love Your Man Even When He Attempts to Kill Your Son*.

It's not just men's and women's ministries, though. We divvy up outreaches by age group. For example, a church may have: Lil' Lambs (babies), Lil' Lions (pre-K), K5 KidZone (elementary), Surge 4 Him (middle school), and Khaos Krew (high school). Or maybe it's time to have all the newlyweds over here (the "Hopeful Promises" small group) and the singles over there (the "You-know-Paul-was-single-too" small group). I recently saw on Twitter the suggestion of "Heaven's Waiting Room" for the older crowd. Yikes!

My point is that we are naturally good at outreaching to segmented groups. Sometimes we need to think through *why* we focus on the group we are ministering to separately. It makes sense why we have a women's ministry and a men's ministry. God has given men and women different bodies, different talents, and different commands. We work in life together, but sometimes it is good to see how other men or other women are handling the stress of life and serving God. We separate the third grader from the high school senior because peer pressure looks different at different ages. We speak differently to a high school student about sexuality and marriage than we do to an eight-year-old.

Part 1: Let No One Despise You

The Babylon Bee is a satirical Christian news site (like *The Onion*, but more Russell Moore jokes). The headline of one article reads "32-Year-Old Forcibly Transferred From College Ministry to Singles' Ministry."[1] Apparently this was done after the individual, Jackson Freeman, had "an impressive 14-year stint in the church's college group." Transitioning into the church's singles' ministry, Freeman joined a group consisting "of over three-dozen single men and five women in their twenties and thirties." Like any good satire, there is a grain of truth here, and I think it's not just about a guy who refuses to grow up, but also about a church *that has no idea what to do with this age group*.

So why do young adults matter? Why should churches put effort, time, and money into college and young adults ministry? Why should young adults bother to engage with their local church? Generally, the reasons break down into two groups. This age group is:

1. Capable of great things.
2. The future (*and present*) of the church.

Capable of Great Things

Consider the ages of the following milestones:

- Joan of Arc led the French in the defeat of the English at the Siege of Orleans at age 17.
- Pele won his first World Cup at age 17.
- Bill Gates co-founded Microsoft at age 19.
- Trevor Bayne was the youngest driver to win the Daytona 500 at age 20.
- Jonathan Edwards was ordained at age 23.
- Ben Roethlisberger became the youngest quarterback to win the Super Bowl at age 23.
- Charles Lindbergh was the first to successfully complete a solo flight across the Atlantic Ocean, at age 25.
- Harriet Tubman escaped from slavery at age 27.

---

1. "32-Yeal-Old Forcibly Transferred."

There are two ways to respond to that list: 1) "I've done nothing with my life," and 2) "Wow that's really inspirational" (for the record, I'm going for the latter).

Sometimes accomplishments are not necessarily attention grabbers like above. I have met some remarkable young people in my time working with college students. I think of one single mom in her early 20s who started classes a month after giving birth and then made the dean's list. Or those who are first-generation college students from families where English is a second language. Some of them are students who get plastered the first week at college, nearly dying from alcohol poisoning, then turn their lives around. It's not just college students, though. Think about the high school grad who immediately entered the work force and now owns her own business with multiple employees by the time she is 25. Or the guy who enlisted in the military and returned home a decorated veteran at the ripe old age of 23. Society and our churches sometimes sell people short on what they are capable of at a younger age, and it needs to stop.

Young people are capable of more than what society often gives credit for. If you do a Google search on "Millennials" (the generation born between 1981 and 1996) you'll find a lot of negative stuff. Millennials demand instant gratification and spend too much time online. They are narcissistic. They grew up with participation trophies. And you know what? Some of that may be true for many Millennials, but *every* generation has its negative stereotypes. Generation X (born 1965–1981) has been called lazy, cynical, and apathetic. Baby Boomers (born 1946–1964) are treated as technophobes who are resistant to change. And before you "Okay, Boomer" me, I was born in 1984.

Further, it's not like the older generations never complained about Boomers or Gen-Xers. That's the unfortunate cycle. While Christians *should* be better at encouraging its young adults than the rest of the world, Millennials and Gen-Zers will probably still encounter these negative attitudes in the church. My advice is to not get too worked up about the stereotypes. Yeah, they're annoying, but if we're being honest there is a good chance our generations will complain a decent amount about the generations that come after us. I'm not defending it, and I hope we can change it, but this has been a common pattern throughout history.

Like the ministries I discussed at the beginning of this chapter, we as a church are too good at dividing people up by their differences. I get the irony of a person writing a book specifically about young people lamenting the segmentation of the Christian population, but I am not saying there is never a good reason to minister specifically to certain social identities. However, when we separate a group and then speak negatively of them and expect little from them, that is not a ministry—it's a mockery.

Challenges for Today's Young Adults

Also keep in mind the specific challenges Christians in this age bracket have faced recently. Many of the young adults who graduated college in the recent past faced historically bad employment. The U.S. unemployment rate spiked to over 7 percent in late 2008 for the first time since 1994. It would peak at 9.3 percent in October of 2009 and not dip below 7 percent again until November of 2013. More recent college graduates are facing a better employment environment (unemployment would dip to as low as 3.5 by September 2019, its lowest since 1969),[2] but years of weak job outlooks for college graduates have lasting effects. Additionally, the 2020 coronavirus outbreak has reversed much of this improvement.

Meanwhile the need for a college degree has increased to absurd levels. A 2013 *Washington Post* article by Catherine Rampell says, "The college degree is becoming the new high school diploma: the new minimum requirement, albeit an expensive one, for getting even the lowest-level job."[3] Rampell shares a story of a Georgia law firm that requires its receptionists, administrative assistants, file clerks, and "even the office 'runner'"—who gets paid $10 an hour—to have a bachelor's degree. Twenty, 15, even 10 years ago, this would seem ridiculous, but welcome to the world of "degree inflation."

It's not going to get better soon. A report from Georgetown Public Policy Institute notes that in 1973, 16 percent of all jobs required at least a bachelor's degree. That number increased to 29 percent in 1992 and to 32 percent in 2010. The report anticipates a rate of 35 percent by 2020. This means over one third of the entire working population will need *at least* a bachelor's degree to find a job in 2020.[4]

Yet earning that bachelor's degree has never been more costly. Including tuition, fees, room, and board, and adjusting for inflation (using 2015 dollars), a public four-year institution averaged $2,387 a year during the 1975–76 school year. By 1985–86 it increased only slightly, to $2,918. By

2. Bureau of Labor Statistics, "Labor Force Statistics."
3. Rampell, "College Degree."
4. Carnevale et al., *Recovery*, 2.

1995–96 it surged to $4,845, and then up to $6,708 in 2005–6. More recently (2015–16) it averaged $9,410. In 1996 it would have cost $17,596 to obtain a bachelor's degree from a four-year public institution. In 2016 it cost $37,640. That's an extra 20 grand for the same degree![5] Even after adjusting for inflation, the cost of tuition at a four-year public institution rose on average 3.1 percent a year from 2008 to 2018.[6]

Some say the higher education bubble is bound to burst much like the housing bubble did. When the housing market collapsed in late 2008, many homeowners found their mortgages "under water." That is, they owed more on the house than what it was worth. For a college degree, this means the debt owed is more than what the degree could likely earn back—despite the increased need for a bachelor's degree in today's job market. Think of being $100,000 in debt and making minimum wage at Starbucks. But instead of owing that money on a liberal arts degree, it's a biochemistry or computer science degree, a degree that should seemingly lead to a great job.

Does this situation sound bleak? Reports show Millenials are feeling especially stressed and depressed. A CBS News article in 2013 reported that "Millennials are more stressed than any other current living generation, according to a new survey conducted by the American Psychological Association and Harris Interactive."[7] The study found that Millennials "had a stress level of 5.4 out of 10." To put that in context, "The researchers generally considered a stress level of 3.6 to be healthy." It was also noted that this statistic counters the overall decrease in stress levels across all older age groups. The same study also predictably reported higher levels of depression among Millennials. As a whole, this generation, which should just be hitting its prime with their lives ahead of them, are anxious and depressed.

Generation Z (those born in 1997 through the mid-2010s[8]) is not fairing any better. *Business Insider* summarized a 2019 Pew Research Center study, noting, "The number of US teens ages 12 to 17 who said they experienced at least one major depressive episode in 2017 increased by 59 percent since 2007. That's a total of 3.2 million teens, or 13 percent of the entire cohort."[9] Additionally, teen girls are "three times as likely as teen boys

---

5. CollegeBoard, "Trends."
6. Martin, "What's the Return."
7. Castillo, "Millennials."
8. Dimock, "Defining Generations."
9. Hoffower, "Depression Is on the Rise among Gen Z."

Part 1: Let No One Despise You

to deal with depression." We're talking about back-to-back generations of increased depression.

A new study from *JAMA Pediatrics* suggests this issue isn't about to resolve itself or fade away. CNN explains, "Spending too much time scrolling through social media and watching more television has been linked with symptoms of depression in young people."[10] Moreover, "For every additional hour young people spend on social media or watching television, the severity of depressive symptoms they experience goes up." It's no secret our world is becoming more digital with much of today's social interaction existing through screens, be it social media or texting. Today's young adults are depressed, and their preferred use of communication is making it worse.

Shane Pruitt explains how Generation Z knows and experiences brokenness at an earlier age than previous generations:

> [Generation Z is] exposed to more violence, graphic images, and evil at an earlier age. Internet exposure, media coverage, and broken homes are unfortunately the norm for far too many. They don't know a world without the fear of mass shootings, and terrorism. This is also pornography-saturated generation—the average age of first exposure is 11. The fastest growing consumer of Internet pornography is girls 15–30; 70% of guys admit to interaction with Internet pornography and 50% of girls. This generation is looking for solutions at a much earlier time in their lives. *They know they're broken. Thank God for the gospel, because it is mighty to save* Gen Z. Share it with them, because they're starving for it, whether they know it or not.[11]

And none of this even addresses the additional chaos young Christians are facing in society. But more on that in chapter 8. Youth are capable of accomplishing remarkable things, but this current crop of youth are facing immense challenges. Suffice to say, the young adults in our churches could use some support, or at the very least, a few less jokes about "snowflake" Millennials. They can do more than what is expected of them.

Future (and Present) of the Church

The other primary reason young people matter is that they are the future of the church. This goes for both the youth already hooked up with a church

---

10. Howard, "Increasing Social Media Use."
11. Pruitt, "7 Common Traits of Gen Z." Emphasis added.

and those who do not know God yet, or even hate God. Russell Moore, president of the Ethics and Religious Liberty Commission, says:

> The next Billy Graham might be drunk right now. The next Jonathan Edwards might be the man driving in front of you with the Darwin Fish bumper decal. The next Charles Wesley might currently be a misogynistic, profanity-spewing hip-hop artist. The next Charles Spurgeon might be managing an abortion clinic today. The next Mother Teresa might be a heroin-addicted porn star this week. The next Augustine of Hippo might be a sexually promiscuous cult member right now, just like, come to think of it, the first Augustine of Hippo was.[12]

The point is that young adult ministry is an all-hands-on-deck opportunity. If you confess Christ, it does not matter if you are a college student, a 20-something, a newly enlisted marine, a nearly retired science professor, a youth pastor, or anything else; you have an incredible and glorious burden to cultivate the future of the church. Not only for the salvation of their own souls, but for the generations that follow.

Thirty years from now we will all be sitting listening to sermons preached by folks that were grafted into the body of Christ one way or another. Paul writes about this same idea in Romans 11 when he speaks about Gentiles being "grafted in" with the Jews who have already accepted Christ. The future of the church and your *local* church depends on Millennials and Gen Z.

To add some encouragement to a chapter that has often been a downer, a recent Barna study indicates Millennials are on some fronts more active in their faith than previous generations (Generation X), when considering *practicing Christians* as opposed to *self-identified Christians*. The report noted 71 percent of Millennial practicing Christians read their Bible in the last seven days compared to only 67 percent of their Generation X counterparts (Boomers were also at 71 percent, by the way). Additionally, 79 percent of Millennial practicing Christians "attended a church service in the past seven days, not including a special event such as a wedding or funeral," while that rate was 77 percent for Generation X practicing Christians. The two groups are also remarkably close on three specific Christians beliefs: "God is the all-powerful, all-knowing, perfect creator of the universe who rules the world today" (Millennial practicing Christians 84 percent, Generation X practicing Christians 85 percent); "The Bible is totally accurate in all of

---

12. Moore, *Onward*, 215.

Part 1: Let No One Despise You

its teachings" (65 percent, 64 percent); and, "I will go to heaven because I confess my sins and accepted Jesus as savior" (72 percent, 70 percent).[13]

These statistics indicate the Millennials in our church are not nearly as lost as many may have been led to believe. Yes, this is just the beliefs of *practicing Christians*, but these are likely the college students and young adults showing up on a random Sunday looking for a church to call home. If they demonstrate beliefs consistent with these findings, then perhaps the future of the church is now.

Young adults in our churches are capable of serving and perhaps even leading in some capacity right now. We need to *expect* young people to contribute to the church. Grant Skeldon, founder of Initiative Network, notes he believes this is a reason for many young adults not sticking around the church. "They don't show up because it wouldn't really matter if they did or didn't. They don't own anything. Nothing is on the line if they're absent."[14]

Most of my professional career has been in the field of student conduct. I regularly meet with students who have in some way made bad choices and broke school policy and have maybe even made a mess of their lives. A major part of my role is to teach them responsibility: to themselves and to others. What is the best way to teach someone responsibility? Give them responsibility. Hold them accountable. Jesus said, "The harvest is plentiful, but the laborers are few" (Luke 10:2). So there is plenty of meaningful work (not "busy work") to do in the church. From volunteering with the youth group to visiting shut-ins to delivering meals to a family in need—there is plenty of meaningful work to go around. As young adults demonstrate their commitment, more challenging work can be distributed.

Young adults cannot be called the future of the church, without acknowledgment they are also the present of the church. "Remember, the younger generation is not [only] the future of the church—if they've been redeemed with the blood of Jesus, then they're the church right now."[15]

Investing in and trusting the next generation is an idea folks have taken for granted going all the way back to the Israelites wandering the desert. God led the Jews out of Egypt in a pretty remarkable fashion. Whether it was the plagues, parting the Red Sea, pillars of cloud and fire, quails, manna, water from the rock, or the defeat of the Amalekites, the Jews saw

---

13. Barna Group, "Snapshot of Faith Practice"
14. Skeldon, *Passion Generation*, 281.
15. Pruitt, "7 Common Traits of Gen Z."

many amazing things. But what happened to the next generation after they *finally* reached the promise land?

> When Joshua dismissed the people, the people of Israel went each to his inheritance to take possession of the land. And the people served the Lord all the days of Joshua, and all the days of the elders who outlived Joshua, who had seen all the great work that the Lord had done for Israel. And Joshua the son of Nun, the servant of the Lord, died at the age of 110 years. And they buried him within the boundaries of his inheritance in Timnath-heres, in the hill country of Ephraim, north of the mountain of Gaash. And all that generation also were gathered to their fathers. And there arose another generation after them who did not know the Lord or the work that he had done for Israel. (Judg 2:5–10)

Joshua and his generation witnessed God's miracles. They knew what it meant to have God deliver this land into their hands. They saw it. They felt it. They experienced it. Their children did not. And, apparently, they were not told much about it. Who is to blame? Mostly the older generation. Our Christian history exists in Scripture and books and now in videos and podcasts. But there is still a need for the wisdom an elder/college student mentorship offers. A pastor/20-something mentorship. A deaconess/recent high school grad mentorship. We need the older generations speaking into the lives of the younger generations, and the younger generations need to be ready and willing to participate.

Francis Chan comments on Caleb after reading Judges 14:10–12:

> At 85, Caleb was as courageous as ever. Rarely do we meet people in their fifties and sixties living by faith, much less people in their eighties. In speaking to young adults throughout America, they tell me of how they would love to be mentored by older people who are living by faith. But they can't find any. Some may be joyful and friendly, but no longer living by faith. Sadly, their lives consist of visiting grandkids and taking vacations. Some are still acquiring more possessions, hoping to make the most of their last few days on earth.
>
> This is the opposite of Caleb. At 85, the end was in sight. He was sprinting for the finish line. He experienced the faithfulness of God throughout this lifetime, and it only made him more courageous as life went on.[16]

---

16. Chan and Chan, *You and Me Forever*, 185–86.

Part 1: Let No One Despise You

Older Christians *need to do something* to invest in the next generation of Christians. So much has been written about Millennials leaving the church. Skeldon points out, "If we're freaking out about all the millennials leaving church right now, how bad do you think it'll be when there's none left to disciple the Z generation?"[17] Instead of cracking jokes about "those lazy/entitled/short-attention/snowflake/[insert unoriginal insult here] Millennials," *disciple them*! If the older generation doesn't, who will? And if the church is missing out on Millennials, who is going to disciple Generation Z (who are already graduating from college)?!

I'm using the terms *mentor* and *disciple* somewhat interchangeably, which many may disagree with. The differences between mentoring and discipling for the Christian is ultimately negligible. When we think of mentoring, we think of someone more experienced looking out for someone with less. They give advice, sure, but it's more about walking with the mentee in life, conveying life experiences, listening to their mentee, crafting goals, and holding the mentee accountable to those goals. Discipleship, for the Christian, is basically the same thing. It's just that *for the Christian*, life experiences, conversations, and goals will naturally include one's faith journey.

Some may argue they are not qualified to mentor or disciple a young adult or college student because of such an age gap. They don't know today's pop culture and are unfamiliar with the latest apps. They wear white New Balance sneakers everywhere. Are cargo shorts still hip? (I'm told they aren't, but oh well). Is a Cardi B a backup sweater? Millennials and Gen-Zers don't need apps, memes, or the Billboard Top 40 for discipleship. In their book *Sharing the Journey of Emerging Adulthood*, Richard R. Dunn and Jana L. Sundene argue factors such as "age, marital status, or career achievement" are not the core of effective disciple-making. Instead, "effectiveness is rooted primarily in a willingness to submit to Christ and an openness to invest intentionally and reflectively in an emerging adult's life."[18] Disciple-making is not about age, worldly success, or cultural relevancy: it's about Christlikeness and commitment.

And this mentoring relationship can actually go both ways a little. Young adults have plenty to teach the older generations. If the church wants to reach Millennials and Gen-Zers, they are going to need to listen to the younger generations. They know the ins and outs of their generations. What questions do the younger generations typically have about Jesus?

---

17. Skeldon, *Passion Generation*, 101.
18. Dunn and Sundene, *Shaping the Journey*, 18.

Where can they be found, physically or digitally? Again, this is why Christian young adults are so important to the present, and not just the future, of the church.

There are many great resources available on discipleship. One I have found useful is Mark Dever's *Discipling: How to Help Others Follow Jesus*. He says, "discipling is not that complicated. It's about doing life together with other people as you all journey toward Christ."[19] This involves finding someone to disciple, establishing goals, and then just disciple them. This relationship requires the disciple to "teach, correct, model, and love" and showing not only one's strengths, but one's weaknesses. It's being transparent and vulnerable. The Great Commission is about making disciples, and I hope our churches prioritize discipling young adults.

There is no excuse to pass this up. If you are a leader in your church, find someone in this age bracket and disciple them. It might be awkward to start, but it's really simple. Here are some sample lines:

> You attend the college in town, right? Would you like to come over to our house for dinner after the service? If not today, can you do next week?
>
> How long have you been coming to [insert church name]? That's great! I've been here about [insert length of time you've been attending/a member]. Would you like to get a cup of coffee some time to talk more about our church and what we believe about Jesus?

Or, if you are a late teen or 20-something going to church but lacking a mentor, find an elder and try to connect with him or have him refer you to someone. Again, maybe a little awkward, so here is an example:

> Hi, you go here, right? I'm kind of new, and I was hoping to talk to someone more about church. Do you know someone?

Matters like schedules and goals will need to be sorted out later, but getting started isn't rocket science, just maybe a little awkward. G. K. Chesterton wrote, "A man who has faith must be prepared not only to be a martyr, but to be a fool." In other words, do not tell God you would die for him if you will not even put up with an awkward conversation or two. Get involved with discipleship, because young adults matter to the church.

---

19. Dever, *Discipling*, 86.

4

Spirit of Immediacy

The gospel message demands a response. A well-worn verse from Revelation says, "So, because you are lukewarm, and neither hot nor cold, I will spit you out of my mouth" (Rev 3:16). The book of Revelation is a vision John has of Jesus in heaven and returning to Earth to establish God's new kingdom. By chapter 3, Jesus is instructing John to write down messages for various churches. In this verse, Jesus is speaking to the church in Laodicea, and I can ensure you it's not an encouraging moment. Jesus admonishes the church for being lukewarm in their faith: they aren't living out their faith; rather, they're just there.

It's kind of like showing up to church . . . *some Sundays*. Or giving money in the collection plate . . . *when you have a few bucks on you*. Or praying before meals . . . *when the pastor is visiting*. By no means am I saying church attendance, tithing, and prayer get to you heaven; that's been accomplished by grace through faith. But we are told that we will recognize a Christ-follower by their fruit (Matt 7:16), and worshipping God in community, living sacrificially, and spending time in prayer are all reasonable indicators of a genuine faith. Doing so on occasion or when you think someone is watching is a lukewarm faith, and Jesus told John such Christians will be rejected.

So, again, the gospel message demands a response. It's not something to put off until one is a little more settled in life. Many emerging adults have been given the impression a commitment to following Christ isn't time sensitive. If you're in college thinking, "I like God, but I really want to party the next few years and the Bible lays too much guilt on me for that. When I graduate, I'll start taking the God thing more seriously," my first response is easy: no, you won't.

Spirit of Immediacy

Think of it this way: the person who takes a puff and says "This is my last cigarette" is less believable than the person who says "Yesterday I smoked my last cigarette." Why is that? The first person says he will stop smoking *while he's smoking*. The second person *is looking back on the act* saying he will change. For the second person, there is at least some level of detachment from the act. It's easy to *say* you'll never do something again *while you're doing it*. There is no risk in that. You're currently enjoying what you want while making an empty promise. Someone who says "I'll follow Jesus after I do whatever I want" really has no interest in following Jesus. They will keep finding new "wants" to address before they turn to Jesus. However, there is hope for the person who the day after a one-night stand or binge drinking says, "I need Jesus."

Kyle Idleman in *Not a Fan* describes being in college and learning of "the 'as now, so then' principle of human behavior." Interestingly, this principle "is the idea that current habits are overwhelmingly the most likely predictor of future practices. The vast majority of the time, the decision you make today will be the decision you make tomorrow. If you don't do it now there is no reason to think you will then."[1]

Habits are easy to form and hard to break. If you are putting off making a change, will you ever change? Consider New Year's resolutions. How often do they work? There is nothing magical about January 1. When it comes down to it, that date is completely arbitrary and means nothing. Someone who truly wants to lose weight won't wait (pun intended) until after the holidays. They will start right away. If you actually want to follow Christ, putting him off until after college probably means you are not interested. The same goes for those of you who are not in college, but are waiting until you get married and have kids to find a local church.

Still, my second response to the "I'll wait to take Jesus seriously later" might be more important: you don't know if you have tomorrow. That's my idea of a *spirit of immediacy*.

Some of you might already understand what I am proposing. You may have experienced what it means to lose someone to death "before their time," whether it was a parent, a sibling, or a friend. Others have only experienced death of someone much older, which is, of course, still sad and heart-wrenching. The first person in my life that I remember dying was our neighbor, Gladys, when I was about 12. She was in her 80s at the time and I was real sad because she was a wonderful person and almost like a

---

1. Idleman, *Not a Fan*, 195–96.

grandmother to me. But she was in her 80s. As sad as her death was, we all grasp the fact that we do not live forever and that once we get to a certain age, our time is pretty limited. It is when someone dies well before they're "supposed to" that we learn what immediacy means. I learned this when I was 17.

In November of 2001 I was a senior in high school. My first-period classes were electives, going from Journalism II one day and some home economics class the next. I had taken a number of journalism classes and developed a great relationship with the teacher. It was the perfect way to start every other day, so I usually arrived to school casually and with little notice of what was going on around me. Except this day.

On this day I arrived to school and saw a lot of people, especially my fellow seniors, in tears. I have a permanently engrained image of one girl in particular sitting on the floor across from a row of lockers, bawling. I quickly found out that the night before a girl in my class, Laura, died in a car crash. It happened at an intersection I passed a thousand times, a block from my old elementary school.

This was the first time I ever experienced the death of someone my own age. I had lost grandparents, neighbors, and other folks close to me, but they were usually in their 70s or 80s. And while it hurts no matter the age, there is at least some level of expectation that as you get older, death gets closer.

I had a number of classes with Laura throughout middle school and high school. The previous spring, she and I took Art History together, and the semester she died I was in an accounting class with her. I don't want to oversell how close I was to Laura. We didn't really run with the same crowds, although our paths occasionally crossed outside of class. When the paths did cross, we talked friendly, genuinely enjoying the conversation. Same in class. We might not have purposefully sought each other out, but if we were in a group together or were assigned to sit near each other, we talked easily and comfortably. Then she was gone.

This isn't a scare tactic. It's real life. People die, and you often don't know it's about to happen. One day someone you know, someone you hang out with, someone you love is in your life, and the next day they are not. And then that's it. Anything you wanted to do with them, anything you wanted to tell them, *it's too late*. That's the importance of immediacy when it comes to faith. That's why putting off following Christ doesn't make sense. If you are mature enough to understand the gospel, you are mature enough to know that you are not promised tomorrow to make the decision. Car wrecks, cancer, homicides, fires, and coronaviruses don't ask permission before taking a life.

I believe Jesus when he says, "I am the way, and the truth, and the life. No one comes to the Father except through me" (John 14:6). I don't know *exactly* what hell looks like, but it's clear it *at least* involves an eternal separation from God, and the only way to avoid that separation is Jesus. I sat at a funeral in November of 2001 as a follower of Christ, not knowing if the teenage girl being laid to rest, the girl I saw in Ms. Bly's accounting class just the week before, knew Jesus. That's what I mean when I say a *spirit of immediacy*. We need to approach this world and our faith with the belief that nothing tomorrow is guaranteed. Our Christian witness, that is, what we share with others about our faith, needs to reflect that. Our own commitment to Christ needs to reflect that.

Immediacy in Scripture

Scripture informs us that what we have in front of us will not always be there. Our lives on Earth are momentary blips on the timeline of history, from "in the beginning" through eternity.

My old pastor, Eric Miller, explains it like this: "Every life on earth, including your own; every empire that has ever existed, or will, is finite and it's fleeting." He then points out that so far Earth has existed for roughly 2.4 million days, that each empire typically lasts 90,000–100,000 days, and that man, living up to 120 years, gets roughly 44,000 days.[2] In the scope of history and eternity, that's not many.

Miller, formerly a math teacher, also once explained it as something like this: our lives on Earth are like line segments, but the lives of our souls are like rays. If you recall from math class, line segments have a definite beginning and a definite end. My line segment starts in 1984 and will end at a time I don't know yet. For this example, let's say 2060 (I would be 76 years old). That line segment represents what I lived here on Earth: a beginning and an end. However, our souls are like rays. It has a definite start, but continues on forever as represented by the arrow at the end of the ray. In this case, my soul began when God started to form me in my mother's womb in 1983, and will continue on without ceasing into eternity. Everyone's ray will travel beyond their earthly death and continue into either an eternity in heaven or an eternity in hell.

2. Miller, *Daniel*.

Part 1: Let No One Despise You

The prophet Isaiah tell us, "All flesh is grass, and all its beauty is like the flower of the field. The Grass withers, the flower fades when the breath of the Lord blows on it; surely the people are grass. The grass withers, the flower fades, but the word of our God will stand forever" (Isa 40:6–8).

James echoes this immediacy when he says, "Come now, you who say, 'Today or tomorrow we will go into such and such a town and spend a year there and trade and make a profit'—yet you do not know what tomorrow will bring. What is your life? For you are a mist that appears for a little time and then vanishes" (Jas 4:13–14).

Our lives on earth are not permanent, and we do not know the expiration date. This is why Paul writes, "Behold, now is the favorable time; behold, now is the day of salvation" (2 Cor 6:2).

Which brings us to the indispensable word "repent." In Greek, the word is *metanoia*, which means "a change in mind." Notice that the word "repent" is a verb; that is, to repent requires action, and the implication is *immediate* action.

Job, after God rebukes him, declares he will "repent in dust and ashes" (Job 42:6). David warns, "If a man does not repent, God will whet his sword" (Ps 7:12). The prophet Ezekiel delivers a message from God that says, "Repent and turn from all your transgressions, lest iniquity be your ruin" (Ezek 18:30).

In the New Testament, John the Baptist is the first to plea for repentance. Remember, his mission was to prepare the way for Jesus, and part of doing so was proclaiming, "Repent of your sins and turn to God, for the Kingdom of Heaven is near" (Matt 3:2, NLT). At the beginning of his ministry, Jesus too says, "The time is fulfilled, and the kingdom of heaven is at hand; repent and believe in the gospel" (Mark 1:15).

Consider what happens in John 8. This is where some Pharisees bring a woman caught in adultery to Jesus, saying she needs to be stoned. Everyone remembers that Jesus tells them, "Let him who is without sin among you be the first to throw a stone at her," and how the accusers all leave and no one is left to condemn the woman. That's an incredible example of forgiveness on Jesus' part! But what happens next? Jesus tells her, "Go, and from now on sin no more" (John 8:11). That's a command to repent, a command to her to change her mind on adultery.

Repentance is an act. It is a turning away from one's sins and sinful life. That doesn't mean we will be perfect, but it signifies our obedience to Christ.

Spirit of Immediacy

Three Specific Examples of Immediacy in Scripture

There are three incredible examples from Scripture that demonstrate this repentance, this *immediacy*, that I want to share.

The first comes from 2 Kings 22:8-20. Some background might be helpful. After Solomon dies, the kingdom of Israel splits into two kingdoms: Israel to the north, and Judah to the south. From this point on, all of Israel's kings find themselves against God, while Judah at least has a couple here and there that honor God. One of these good kings was Josiah.

During his reign, the high priest gives Josiah's secretary a book that he found: "the Book of the Law in the house of the Lord." Basically, this book was lost over time and contained instructions from God. There had been so many terrible leaders and people who did not love God that no one bothered to pass the information along. When his secretary read from the book, Josiah "tore his clothes" in agony. He knew they had gone astray, and he was fearful, "For great is the wrath of the Lord that is kindled against us, because our fathers have not obeyed the words of this book." It was an *immediate* response. Now, Josiah was right; God was angry at how his people had turned against him. However, in response to Josiah's repentance, God mercifully declared:

> But to the king of Judah, who sent you to inquire of the Lord, thus shall you say to him, Thus says the Lord, the God of Israel: Regarding the words that you have heard, because your heart was penitent, and you humbled yourself before the Lord, when you heard how I spoke against this place and against its inhabitants, that they should become a desolation and a curse, and you have torn your clothes and wept before me, I also have heard you, declares the Lord. Therefore, behold, I will gather you to your fathers, and you shall be gathered to your grave in peace, and your eyes shall not see all the disaster that I will bring upon this place. (2 Kgs 22:18-20)

Judah was in for some rough days, but Josiah's repentance spared him from God's wrath.

In a second example, Matthew 4:18-22 shows Jesus calling one third of his disciples, all busy fishing at the time. We first read about brothers Peter and Andrew casting nets into the sea. Jesus says to them, "Follow me, and I will make you fishers of men." What is the response? "*Immediately* they left their nets and followed him." Continuing on, Jesus comes across another pair of brothers, James and John, mending nets with their father. Jesus calls them to follow, and "*Immediately* they left the boat and their father and followed him."

Part 1: Let No One Despise You

Notice the complete lack of hesitation. Jesus approaches two different sets of brothers with the same proposition: ditch what you're doing in life, and follow me. And both times the word "immediately" is used to describe them walking away from whatever life they had planned in order to follow Jesus.

The final story I'd like to share on this point is about Philip from Acts 8:26–38. In the early church, issues arose regarding inequitable treatment of widows and orphans between the Jews and Hellenistic (Greek) Jews. To resolves this, the disciples chose seven additional believers to help serve others. Think of them as the first deacons. Philip was one of those individuals. Instead of summarizing this particular story, here it is in its entirety:

> Now an angel of the Lord said to Philip, "Rise and go toward the south to the road that goes down from Jerusalem to Gaza." This is a desert place. And he rose and went. And there was an Ethiopian, a eunuch, a court official of Candace, queen of the Ethiopians, who was in charge of all her treasures. He had come to Jerusalem to worship and was returning, seated in his chariot, and he was reading the prophet Isaiah. And the Spirit said to Philip, "Go over and join this chariot." So Philip ran to him and heard him reading Isaiah the prophet and asked, "Do you understand what you are reading?" And he said, "How can I, unless someone guides me?" And he invited Philip to come up and sit with him. Now the passage of the Scripture that he was reading was like this:
>
> "Like a sheep he was led to the slaughter
> and like a lamb before its shearer is silent,
> so he opens not his mouth.
> In his humiliation justice was denied him.
> Who can describe his generation?
> For his life is taken away from the earth."
>
> And the eunuch said to Philip, "About whom, I ask you, does the prophet say this, about himself or about someone else?" Then Philip opened his mouth, and beginning with this Scripture he told him the good news about Jesus. And as they were going along the road they came to some water, and the eunuch said, "See, here is water! What prevents me from being baptized?" And he commanded the chariot to stop, and they both went down into the water, Philip and the eunuch, and he baptized him. (Acts 8:26–38)

Talk about immediacy! Philip is instructed to approach this Ethiopian and explain the gospel. As the two travel the desert, they come to some small body of water. An oasis? A stream? A puddle? Who knows? The Ethiopian, recognizing the importance of this message and not wanting to miss his opportunity, exclaims, "Here is water! What prevents me from being baptized?" In this moment, the Ethiopian went for it. The gospel message demanded a response, and the Ethiopian was unambiguous. If you are still sitting on the fence with this Jesus stuff, what is it that prevents you from going all in?

Youth Is No Obstacle to Christ

The truth is that when you're called by Christ, you're called by Christ. God doesn't seem interested in whatever excuse you have, including "I'm too young" or "I'm not ready."

I think we all look for excuses to put off following Christ. If not a large-scale, "I'm not a Christian" rejection, at least a smaller "I'm not a Christian *in this moment*" rejection. Using one's age as an excuse seems to be one of the dumber excuses. It's an excuse that can only last so long. While youth may be relative, at one point or another it ends: whether it's that first Social Security check or an obituary, you will not be young forever. Someone using youth as an excuse to not follow Christ should just drop the charade and either commit to Christ or be honest about their real hesitations.

Jeremiah tried this excuse with God. Spoiler alert: it didn't work. In the first chapter of the book of Jeremiah, we read his response to God's call:

Now the word of the Lord came to me, saying,

"Before I formed you in the womb I knew you,
and before you were born I consecrated you;
I appointed you a prophet to the nations."

Then I said, "Ah, Lord God! Behold, I do not know how to speak, for I am only a youth." But the Lord said to me,

"Do not say, 'I am only a youth':
for to all whom I send you, you shall go,
and whatever I command you, you shall speak.
Do not be afraid of them,
for I am with you to deliver you,
declares the Lord."

Then the Lord put out his hand and touched my mouth. And the Lord said to me,

Part 1: Let No One Despise You

> "Behold, I have put my words in your mouth.
> See, I have set you this day over nations and over kingdoms,
> to pluck up and to break down,
> to destroy and to overthrow,
> to build and to plant." (Jer 1:4–10)

A few verses later, God continued with these instructions and warnings to Jeremiah:

> But you, dress yourself for work; arise, and say to them everything that I command you. Do not be dismayed by them, lest I dismay you before them. And I, behold, I make you this day a fortified city, an iron pillar, and bronze walls, against the whole land, against the kings of Judah, its officials, its priests, and the people of the land. They will fight against you, but they shall not prevail against you, for I am with you, declared the Lord, to deliver you. (Jer 1:17–19)

God's call of Jeremiah starts pretty simply, essentially saying: "Jeremiah, I know you, and I have a job for you." We often use this scripture to argue for a pro-life stance, which is absolutely fine, but let us not just project this verse onto the value of another's life. Let us also use it to justify the value God has placed on our own lives. He knows you (identity), and he has a job for you (purpose).

Jeremiah tries to make the excuse that he is too young. After all, he doesn't know all the right words. People might not take him seriously. What if he messes up? What if people reject him? God quickly answers by telling Jeremiah that the words he will speak aren't Jeremiah's, but his own.

Jeremiah's call is less about Jeremiah, and more about God. It's not that we shouldn't look for ways to serve God and do great things, but when we recognize that God is on his throne and will equip us for whatever he instructs us to do, we realize that it's not about us, it's about God. Jeremiah needed to be reminded of this fact. He wasn't being sent without the One who sent him.

A more recent birthdate is not an impediment to God. He created you and is keenly aware of your age. If God is raising you up to be his servant, your "I'm only 20 years old" excuse to him will likely be met with an "I know." Youth is not an excuse.

5

A Brief Word of Caution

We need to end this first section with some temperance. The overall goal so far has been to encourage young people to follow and serve Christ in big ways without concern over their age. Individuals like Timothy and Jeremiah were both called to service at a young age, even if only young relatively speaking. When God calls, he does so without any concern regarding whatever obstacle you see. This means, in terms of service to Christ, age becomes irrelevant. None of this, however, means one should ignore their elders.

Respect Authority

I have one of those Bibles with really big margins so you can add notes next to Scripture. I can be wordy or long-winded, so it's pretty much a necessity. If you flip through my Bible, you will see some places where I have a couple paragraphs of my thoughts and responses to selections of Scripture. Next to Titus 3:3 I have simply written: "This one is tough for me." What does Titus 3:3 say? "Remind them to be submissive to rulers and authorities."

Inherently, I'm a contrarian. That's a fancy way of saying I like to disagree and challenge people. It can be a good quality, because it partially means that I am not okay with the status quo. I do not like accepting things just because they are the way they are. You and I can both recognize things in our world, in our country, and in our local community that are messed up. We should not be afraid to speak out against them. However, this personality trait makes it difficult to be submissive, and the Bible is all about

Part 1: Let No One Despise You

submission: submitting to God first and foremost, but also counting ourselves as lesser than others. In Mark 9:35 Jesus tells his disciples, "If anyone would be first, he must be last of all and servant of all." That's hard to do when you always think you are right.

It is not an easy thing to submit to rulers. Some of us seem naturally rebellious to our parents, to our church leaders, or to our governments. I know I can be guilty of this. It's sinful, because clearly we are to obey authorities unless they coerce us to do something against our service to Christ.

Jesus talked about this when the Pharisees sent some people to try to trick him in front of everyone. They asked Jesus about paying taxes, and whether doing so was honoring Caesar (the ruling authority) over God. If Jesus said "Pay your taxes," it signaled man's authority over God. If he said "Don't pay your taxes," they could have alerted the Romans that Jesus was subverting their authority. Jesus knew they were trying to trap him, and Matthew 22 describes the ordeal like this: "But Jesus, aware of their malice, said, 'Why put me to the test, you hypocrites? Show me the coin for the tax.' And they brought him a denarius. And Jesus said to them, 'Whose likeness and inscription is this?' They said, 'Caesar's.' Then he said to them, "Therefore render to Caesar the things that are Caesar's and to God the things that are God's'" (Matt 22:18–21).

Jesus' answer to these would-be hustlers walked the line: if it's God's, give it God; if it's man's, give it to man and man's authority. These coins were stamped with Caesar's countenance, and there is nothing wrong with that. Money is, like many things, an entity capable of being used for good or for evil. Money is an alternative to a bartering system. We as a society voluntarily agree our paper or coin currency is worth a certain amount among each other and trade it for goods and services. Without money, we are left trying to figure out how many pigs a new dishwasher is worth. Without money and the ability to work to earn it, we are left with a society that plunders and steals from each other to gain wealth. My point is that money is neither good nor bad, and Jesus recognizes that.

Physical money is not something directly from God, though he clearly calls us to sacrifice and to give to the needy. Since it is a human creation, humanity can ask for it back. This does not interfere with our worship of God and we should pay our taxes, even though we do not want to and may even refer to it as legalized theft.

It is not just governing authorities we are to submit to, though. Scripture makes it pretty clear that we are to obey our parents. It is, after all, the fifth commandment (Exod 20:12). Paul reminds us of this submissive relationship in Ephesians, writing, "Children, obey your parents in the Lord, for this is right" (Eph 6:1).

Being a bold young person committed to Christ is not a license to be disrespectful of one's parents, even if a parent is a non-believer. Of course, there are circumstances where one may have to go against his or her parents, but those examples are few and far in between. If a parent tells you to stop going to church, rebel and go to church. If a parent throws away your Bible, get another one. However, just because you *don't like* what your parents say does not mean you go against it. Only do this when your parents are instructing something counter to God's commands. Admittedly, honoring one's parents can become more complicated as emerging adults grow up, move out of the house, and have their own families.

We are also all called to be under the authority of our church elders. "Likewise, you who are younger, be subject to the elders. Clothe yourselves, all of you, with humility toward one another, for 'God opposes the proud but gives grace to the humble'" (1 Pet 5:5).

Again, the obvious caveat is that if any of your elders or pastors instruct you to do anything contrary to biblical teaching, do not do it. An elder who cajoles you to gossip about a situation that has nothing to do with him should be resisted. A youth pastor making sexual advances towards you should be resisted and brought to the attention of parents, church leaders, and law enforcement.

Where Does Wisdom Come From?

And of course the ultimate authority to submit to is the source of all wisdom. Psalm 119:9 clearly lays it out: "How can a young man keep his way pure? By guarding it according to your word." In other words, do you want to make sure you're doing the right thing? Study Scripture and do what it says. Don't get me wrong; it's not easy, but it is simple.

The simplicity is repeated in Proverbs 1:7, where we are instructed, "The fear of the Lord is the beginning of knowledge; fools despise wisdom and instruction." Again, do you want to do the right thing? See God on his throne and serve him. You might get some things wrong here and there, but humbling yourself before God is always a good place to start.

Which is why Paul teaches, "The foolishness of God is wiser than men, and the weakness of God is stronger than men" (1 Cor 1:25). Young or otherwise, we do not know what we are doing apart from God. There is plenty of guidance and wisdom in the Bible if we are only willing to set aside our own prejudices, assumptions, and biases in order to just listen.

Still unsure? James guides us: "If any of you lacks wisdom, let him ask God, who gives generously to all without reproach, and it will be given him. But let him ask in faith, with no doubting" (Jas 1:5–6). Do you lack wisdom? Ask God for some. He has plenty. Be sure to ask knowing he is capable of granting it.

My words of caution are out of the way. Your young age is not an obstacle to serving Christ and leading in the church. No one should despise you because of your age.

On the other hand, there is a good chance the world will, in fact, despise you just for being a Christian.

Part 2

You Will Be Hated

6

Whatever Happened to Timothy?

We started together examining Timothy's ministry and his relationship with Paul. Timothy was on the ground floor of the early Christian church and helped spread the gospel throughout Asia and the Mediterranean. He set an example as to how a young adult could further the gospel message. So whatever happened to him? *Foxe's Book of Martyrs* explains, "Timothy was the celebrated disciple of St. Paul, and bishop of Ephesus, where he zealously governed the Church until A.D. 97."

Okay, so far so good. Then what happened?

> At this period, as the pagans were about to celebrate a feast called Catagogion. Timothy, meeting the procession, severely reproved them for their ridiculous idolatry, which so exasperated the people that they fell upon him with their clubs, and beat him in so dreadful a manner that he expired of the bruises two days later.[1]

Well that escalated quickly.

You might ask something like "Why did he let people despise him?" or "Why didn't he live his best life now?" Well, the truth is that Timothy was hardly alone in this kind of experience. In fact, it was downright common at the time.

Here is the fate of a number of early Christians:

> Stephen: Stoned; first Christian martyr
> James, son of Zebedee: Killed by a sword as ordered by Herod
> Andrew: Crucified in Patras (Greece)
> Thomas: Speared in India

1. Foxe, *Foxe's Book of Martyrs*, 11.

Part 2: You Will Be Hated

Philip: Tortured then crucified after converting a city official's wife
Matthias: Either crucified or stoned then beheaded
Peter: Crucified in Rome around 66 AD under Emperor Nero
John: Lived to an old age, but exiled on Patmos (a Greek island)
Justin Martyr: Beheaded in Rome under Marcus Aurelius for not sacrificing to idols
Origen: Imprisoned and tortured; died from injuries related to the torture

This was the world the early Christians lived in. They were not accepted. They were beaten, jailed, exiled, and killed. This was their normal. Yet the gospel was preached and more people began to follow Christ's teachings anyway. In the first section we talked about not letting people despise you for your youth. While that is true, it is mostly a message for inside the Church. Pastors, elders, and parents should not have low expectations for young adults. However, Scripture reverberates with the prospect of persecution. I have been amazed at how many conversations I've had with young adult Christians who have heard strikingly little about the persecution of Christ's bride, the church. If you dedicate your life to Christ, expect to experience it in some level.

You Will be Hated

Here is the key scripture for part two of this book:

> As he sat on the Mount of Olives, the disciples came to him privately, saying, "Tell us when will these things be, and what will be the sign of your coming and of the end of the age?" And Jesus answered them, "See that no one leads you astray. For many will come in my name, saying, 'I am the Christ,' and they will lead many astray. And you will hear of wars and rumors of wars. See that you are not alarmed, for this must take place, but the end is not yet. For nation will rise against nation, and kingdom against kingdom, and there will be famines and earthquakes in various places. All these are but the beginning of the birth pains.
>
> "Then they will deliver you up to tribulation and put you to death, and you will be hated by all nations for my name's sake. And then many will fall away and betray one another and hate one another. And many false prophets will arise and lead many astray. And because lawlessness will be increased, the love of many will grow cold. But the one who endures to the end will be saved. And this gospel of the kingdom will be proclaimed throughout the

whole world as a testimony to all nations, and then the end will come." (Matt 24:3–14)

We sometimes hear or read things that tell us if we truly love God, everything will be easy. That life will *always* be rainbows, coffee at sunrise, and campfires at sunset, listening to John Piper or Al Mohler podcasts while jogging, or Instagramming pics while feeling #blessed. That is a lie from the depths of hell. Spend time in Scripture and this should be obvious. Read history and this should be obvious. Yes, those moments feed our souls and are beautiful, but that is not *always* life. It can't be. If you are a Christian and do not face some levels of persecution in your life, some sort of pushback, some moments of feeling struck down, then you are not living the Christian life. Period.

Now please do not twist these words. *I am not* telling you to pick fights, to scream at people, or to be a jerk. I *am* telling you that living for Christ will naturally result in various forms of persecution. Maybe really small stuff, like a rude comment from someone walking by as you pray before lunch in the dining hall. Maybe really big stuff, like being killed. Or, more likely, something in between. This section will review the many forms persecution takes.

No, Seriously, You Will Be Hated

Not convinced you will be hated for being a Christian from just one passage of Scripture?

> Blessed are you when others revile you and persecute you and utter all kinds of evil against you falsely on my account. Rejoice and be glad, for your reward is great in heaven, for so they persecuted the prophets who were before you. (Matt 5:11–12)

> Do you not know that friendship with the world is enmity with God? Therefore whoever wishes to be a friend of the world makes himself an enemy of God. (Jas 4:3–4)

> Do not love the world or the things in the world. If anyone loves the world, the love of the Father is not in him. For all that is in the world—the desires of the flesh and the desires of the eyes and pride in possessions—is not from the Father but is from the world. And the world is passing away along with its desires, but whoever does the will of God abides forever. (1 John 2:15–17)

Part 2: You Will Be Hated

> Do not be surprised, brothers, that the world hates you. (1 John 3:13)

Jesus, James, and John agree: if you follow Christ, you will be unpopular because of it.

First and foremost, we need to acknowledge that many of us in the United States have experienced very little of this. For years it has been easy to avoid pushback on our faith if we really wanted to. That is changing. Whether it's politics and government, the media, the arts, education institutions, or pretty much anywhere else in our culture, it is becoming less and less popular to be a Christian—particularly a Christian who actually believes the words (all of them) found in the Bible.

For the Christian, this is not a call to retreat, but to push forward even more boldly. F. F. Bruce wrote that it may be tempting to seek comfort and "construct for ourselves right little, tight little encampments, to build walls inside which we feel at home, psychologically insulated from the world outside." But to do such would mock our call to make disciples. Bruce continues, saying, "The world outside . . . is desperately in need of our unchanging Christ. We too must reckon with the fact that, while we are heirs of the kingdom that cannot be shaken, we have here no lasting city and Christ is still calling us forth to occupy fresh territory in his name."[2]

There is expected tension between Christianity and the world, but the world needs Christ and Christians are the ones called to proclaim him to the world.

The World Will Hate You

All this Scripture so far refers to something we often call "the world." You may find the term ambiguous. J. I. Packer explains that when we speak about "the world" we "sometimes mean what it means in the Old Testament, namely, this earth," which God created. However, Packer continues, noting, "Usually . . . it means mankind as a whole, now fallen into sin and moral disorder and become radically anti-God and evil."[3]

For our purposes, we are going to define "the world" like this: our physical, earthly home outside of the spiritual home we have with God through Christ and guided by the Holy Spirit. As Christians, we understand

---

2. Bruce, *Message of the New Testament*, 81.
3. Packer, *Concise Theology*, 234.

that what we see in front of us (this book, the chair you are sitting on, the tree outside your window, your own physical body) is not permanent. This concept was briefly discussed in chapter 4, but let us now expand on it.

In Matthew 24 Jesus is teaching about the end of times; that is, when this physical world will be no more. During this lesson, he states in verse 35, "Heaven and earth will pass away, but my words will not pass away." The implication is that there are physical things that will no longer exist as we know it, with our earthly home being one of them. (Jesus says something similar in Matthew 5:18.)

John warns us to "not love the world or the things in the world. If anyone loves the world, the love of the Father is not in him. For all that is in the world—desires of the flesh and the desires of the eyes and pride of life—is not from the father but is from the world. And the world is passing away along with its desires, but whoever does the will of God abides forever" (1 John 2:15–17). Again, this world is "passing away" and our connection to it ought to be minimal. We should not hold on too tightly to the physical things of this world; nor should we place too high a priority on pleasing the powers of this world.

When writing about his Revelation, John shares this part of his vision:

> Then I saw a new heaven and a new earth, for the first heaven and the first earth had passed away, and the sea was no more. And I saw the holy city, new Jerusalem, coming down out of heaven from God, prepared as a bride adorned for her husband. And I heard a loud voice from the throne saying, "Behold, the dwelling place of God is with man. He will dwell with them, and they will be his people, and God himself will be with them as their God. He will wipe away every tear from their eyes, and death shall be no more, neither shall there be mourning, nor crying, nor pain anymore, for the former things have passed away. (Rev 21:1–4)

Scripture reiterates again and again that there is a spiritual world and a physical world. So the question is, which is our home? Jesus, speaking to his Father about the disciples, says:

> I have given them your word, and the world has hated them because they are not of the world, just as I am not of the world. I do not ask that you take them out of the world, but that you keep them from the evil one. They are not of the world, just as I am not of the world. Sanctify them in the truth; your word is truth. As you sent me into the world, so I have sent them into the world. And for

their sake I consecrate myself, that they also may be sanctified in truth. (John 17: 14–19)

Later, when being examined by Pilate just before being crucified, Jesus explains to him, "My kingdom is not of this world. If my kingdom were of this world, my servants would have been fighting, that I might not be delivered over to the Jews. But my kingdom is not from the world" (John 18:36).

So if Jesus' kingdom is not of this world and we are co-heirs with Christ (Rom 8:17), our kingdom is also not of this world. Paul puts it this way: "Our citizenship is in heaven" (Phil 3:20). What is a citizen? It is not just someone who lives in a certain district, town, or country. It is someone who *legally* lives there, meaning they are afforded particular rights. Adult citizens in the United States have the right to exercise free speech, to expect due process in the legal system, and to vote, among other things. We get this just for being citizens.

Meanwhile, Paul says our real citizenship is in heaven. As Christians, our true home is with God and we have access to all he offers. So when we talk about "the world" we are talking about what we have here on Earth. And to be honest, we should readily give it all up for what God offers.

Who's Running This World Anyway?

To understand who is in charge of this world, we have to go back to the beginning. As in, "in the beginning." Genesis 1:26–28 reads:

> Then God said, "Let us make man in our image, after our likeness. And let them have dominion over the fish of the sea and over the birds of the heavens and over the livestock and over all the earth and over every creeping thing that creeps on earth." So God created man in his own image, in the image of God he created him; male and female he created them. And God blessed them. And God said to them, "Be fruitful and multiply and fill the earth and subdue it, and have dominion over the fish of the sea and over the birds of the heavens and over every living thing that moves on the earth.

God created a world where he put man in charge to steward creation. We have been given such a dominion. In Genesis 2:15 God assigns Adam the task of working and keeping the garden of Eden. Later in the chapter, God gives man Eve to help him with this responsibility. So again, we as humans, under God's authority, were placed in charge to care for the physical world. But what happened? Satan entered the scene. In Genesis 3 we read about the fall, where Adam and Eve disobey God. By disobeying God's command, they forfeit their home in Eden and their dominion over the world. Instead, the woman is cursed with labor pains and the man is cursed to work the land.

While God always remains sovereign and in full authority, man's sin allows another ruler to take his place. Jeff Vanderstelt explains it like this:

> When the Bible speaks of "the world as an enemy," it is not referring to the blue and green rotating ball called Earth that we live on. The world that both James and John warn us about is the place where the rule and reign of the Devil is expressed and experienced (Jas 4:4; 1 John 2:15–17). Satan is called the god of this world, referring to his evil reign of darkness and destruction. In this case, the world is everything that stands against the rule and reign of God.[4]

While it is only authority granted by God, and granted temporarily, Satan from Genesis 3 onward rules the Earth. This is reiterated in Luke 4. The Spirit has drawn Jesus to the wilderness, and then Satan visits, tempting Jesus over the course of 40 days. Versus 5–7 read, "The devil led him up to a high place and showed him in an instant all the kingdoms of the world. And he said to him, 'I will give you all their authority and splendor; it has been given to me, and I can give it to anyone I want to. If you worship me, it will all be yours'" (NIV).

Jesus' response is to quote Deuteronomy 6:13: to serve only God. Noticeably absent is a rebuke on Satan's ability to even offer such a thing. This passage implicitly informs us that Satan, albeit temporarily and only under the authority of God, has control of this world.

Meanwhile, Paul writes in Romans 5:12–14 "Therefore, just as sin came into the world through one man, and death through sin, and so death spread to all men because all sinned—for sin indeed was in the world before the law was given, but sin is not counted where there is no law. Yet death reigned from Adam to Moses, even over those sinning was not like the transgression of Adam, who was a type of the one who was to come."

And in then in Galatians 1:3–5 he says, "Grace to you and peace from God our Father and the Lord Jesus Christ, who gave himself for our sins to deliver us from the present evil age, according to the will of our God and Father, to whom be the glory forever and ever. Amen."

Both the Romans and Galatians passages above speak to a world that has been overwhelmed with sin and death. We know that there is no sin

---

4. Vanderstelt, *Gospel Fluency*, 104.

in God; therefore this world, in its current form, cannot be *of* God. Yes, God created this world, but he has given it in its present state up to man's sin—sin that entered this world through Satan's temptation of Adam and Eve. Further, Scripture informs us (notably Isa 65:17 and Rev 21:1) that a *new* heaven and a *new* Earth will be formed. Take this to mean the current world has been tainted by sin, death, and Satan's rule, and therefore must be replaced with a new one.

I know it is counterintuitive to think of Satan being in charge of this world. John Piper explains, "In his sovereignty, God considered it wise, as part of his curse on the world after the fall of Adam and Eve, to give Satan a huge power in this world." That's not the end of it, though, because Satan "doesn't have ultimate power . . . God is God, not Satan. Satan's not God. All Satan's power is by permission. He has not autonomy to do anything God does not permit for infinitely wise purposes."[5]

So What Does This All Mean?

Why would I take so much time to discuss how bad this world is? Because we all need a wake-up call, especially those of us who are Christians in America. Most our lives have too much comfort. If we read Scripture, we should have scales fall from our eyes in recognition of what following Christ costs. Whether it is Timothy, Peter, Stephen, Origen, or Jesus himself, the roots of our Christian faith reach deep into the soil of bloody sacrifice. For them, it cost lives. For others, freedom. Or comfort. Or money. Or a relationship. Or any other number of things. In his book *Not a Fan*, Kyle Idleman asks, "Am I really carrying a cross if there is no suffering and sacrifice?" He further questions:

> When is the last time that following Jesus cost you something? When is the last time it cost you a relationship? When is the last time following Jesus cost you a promotion? When is the last time it cost you a vacation? When is the last time you were mocked for your faith? Forget about having our lives threatened . . . When is the last time you went without a meal for the sake of the gospel? Can you really say you are carrying your cross if it hasn't cost you anything? Take a second and answer that question in your mind. Has it cost you anything? If there is no sacrifice involved, if you're

---

5. Piper, "How Much Authority" (podcast episode).

not at least a little uncomfortable, then there is a good chance that you aren't carrying a cross.[6]

Jesus tells us in Matthew 16:24 that we must deny ourselves, pick up our crosses, and follow him. Is there something you need to deny yourself in order to carry a cross?

---

6. Idleman, *Not a Fan*, 161.

7

What Is Persecution?

The English word *persecute* means "to harass or punish in a manner designed to injure, grieve, or afflict; *specifically*: to cause to suffer because of belief."[1] This word has only been around since the mid-fifteenth century. The New Testament Greek word used is *dioko*. *Strong's Concordance* explains this word in its negative sense as to "hunt down."[2] So when we think of persecution, we are thinking of one or more persons going after as to punish one or more persons, typically because of a belief. For persecuted Christians, that's the belief of Jesus as the Son of God and salvation of mankind.

A lack of persecution on any group of Christians is an anomaly in history. Everett Ferguson, a scholar on early Christianity, gives this helpful background:

> Persecution did not begin with the Roman authorities. The New Testament writings tell of fratricidal strife between Jews and Christians, the latter challenging the Jews by claiming to be "the New Israel." In the early chapters of Acts, Stephen (7:57) and James, the brother of John the disciple (12:2), became victims of the Jerusalem mob and of King Herod Agrippa, respectively. Indeed, the writer of Luke-Acts appears to go out of his way to reassure the Roman authorities of the loyalty and general value of the Christians and the hostility of the Jews toward them.
>
> The persecutors and their motives changed in A.D. 64. On July 19 that year a great fire engulfed much of Rome; only four of the fourteen quarters of the city escaped damage. Suspicion

1. *Merriam-Webster*, "Persecute."
2. BibleHub, "Dioko."

What Is Persecution?

immediately fell on Emperor Nero: was this a madcap way of clearing part of the city to make room for new, magnificent streets and buildings in his honor? Nero, however, managed to deflect blame first, apparently, on the Jews, who had a reputation for large-scale arson but also had friends at court; and then onto the Christians. Many Christians (perhaps including Peter) were seized, tortured, and done to death in the arena.[3]

It does not take long for the persecution of Christians to take root. The next couple centuries would see ups and downs for Christians. Sometimes they were left alone; other times their "superstition" or "atheism" would not be tolerated by Rome.

In 303 AD the Diocletianic Persecution began. This was a time period where full persecution of Christians under Roman rule took place. Legal rights were stripped away and countless martyrs were made. This would continue until the Edict of Milan in 313 AD.

Why do I share this? We need to emphasize that as Christians in America, and the West in general, we are the inconsistency. Facing minimal pushback on our faith is the glitch in history and not what the Bible tells us to expect. We have had it pretty easy for a pretty long time. Yet the society young adult Christians in the United States and other Western nations are entering is not as welcoming as previous generations. This is why it is important to recognize persecution is not all or nothing, but a gradient.

Five Stages of Religious Persecution

In 2014, Charles Pope, a Catholic priest, wrote an insightful piece titled "Five Stages of Religious Persecution." This analysis will play the backdrop for the next couple of chapters. Pope identified the following five stages:[4]

1. Stereotyping the targeted group
2. Vilifying the targeted group for alleged crimes or misconduct
3. Marginalizing the targeted group's role in society
4. Criminalizing the targeted group or its work
5. Persecuting the targeted group outright

---

3. Ferguson, "Persecution in the Early Church," 27.
4. Pope, "Five Stages."

Part 2: You Will Be Hated

The point here is to stop thinking in binary terms. Persecution is not black and white. If we think in binary terms, we are likely to lump together things that do not belong together. For example, some of us might feel being told our Christian fellowship can no longer meet on campus is persecution. However, in the Middle East, ISIS is systematically killing Christians and destroying artifacts related to their existence. Clearly the latter scenario is worse, and it seems inappropriate to compare the two. Does that mean the Christian fellowship did not experience persecution? Of course not.

Baylor University professor George Yancey has provided critical insight to this topic, as he himself struggled to determine what is and is not persecution. Readily acknowledging that Christians face discrimination in America today, he balks at calling it persecution, "in light of the harassment of all religions in China, the Holocaust in Nazi Germany, and the oppression of Christians in ancient Rome."[5] However, he also points out how the discrimination American Christians face fits the actual definition of *persecution*. He explains, "One does not have to be thrown into jail or have one's life threatened to be persecuted. Indeed, according to one definition, rude names qualify."

Yet Yancey still understandably distances himself from categorizing what Americans face as *persecution*. He explains, "There is evidence that anti-Christian hate can lead to discrimination. Is it persecution?"[6] Yancey confesses this is a complex and nuanced question and that by a "*clinical* definition . . . Christians are persecuted in the United States." On the other hand, although it fits the definition, culturally *persecution* comes with many preconceived notions. Therefore, he "still discourage[s] Christians in the United States from saying they are persecuted, since what we face today isn't what most people envision when they think of persecution. However, as Christians we should be aware that anti-Christian discrimination is real."

This nuance is why I believe if we see persecution as a gradient, we can have a more informed conversation about the persecution Christians face domestically and abroad. So I think we need to do two things simultaneously: first, we need to understand even basic pushbacks against our faith is technically persecution; second, we should be extremely hesitant to classify to the outside world Msgr. Pope's early stages of persecution as

---

5. Yancey, "What Is Persecution?"
6. Yancey, "Is There Really Anti-Christian Discrimination?"

What Is Persecution?

such. Msgr. Pope writes, "Indeed, here in the States it is rare that a respected segment of American life would become vilified and hated overnight. The usual transformation from respect to vilification progresses in stages that grow in intensity."

Persecution is like a white-to-black gradient.

Figure 1 is an example of a white-to-black gradient. Looking in the utmost top left corner, it's clear that the image is white. Meanwhile, in the bottom right corner, it is clear that the image is black. This is how we should view persecution. Think of the top left as walking down the street past individuals while holding your Bible and arriving to your destination without incident. No one says anything, no one gives you a dirty look, and no one is calling the police on you. Now, consider the bottom right corner confessing your faith in Christ and then being executed. The two situations could not be more different, but persecution can occur in the grey area in between. In fact, there are different shades of grey (I'm not sure if it's more or less than 50). Humans do not naturally like grey areas because it requires critical thinking, analysis, and potentially contemplating multiple points of view. However, most of us experience grey areas regularly.

We Were Made to Suffer

Here is the hard truth that needs to be heard: if you call yourself a Christian, you *cannot* live a life entirely free from persecution as it is defined.

Part 2: You Will Be Hated

That white area in the gradient may seem comfortable, but it is about as metaphorically far from God as you can be. If you are not putting yourself in a position where you may be harassed, afflicted, injured, or suffer (possibly even to the point of death), I would argue your faith is not in Christ. It may be in civil religion, Christian institutions, or a twisted version of God, but not Jesus.

Now do not take that to mean something that is not being said. Especially note that I am not saying: picking theological fights with people and getting cursed at in response is a demonstration of faith; nor does purposefully making yourself suffer bring you closer to God.

To the first point, we are to be salt and light to the world, not arsenic and a flamethrower. Salt and arsenic may both change the taste of a dish, but one kills. A light and a flamethrower will get rid of darkness, but one kills. Facebook commenting, Twitter arguments, and calling in to talk radio tends to bring out the worst in us. If you pick a fight with someone to prove them wrong instead of sharing the gospel to save their soul, you are doing it wrong. And if you are a jerk and someone responds in kind, *do not* claim persecution—they are just mimicking your behavior.

As far as the second point goes, we do not strive towards suffering, we strive towards Christ. Believe it or not, some will make their suffering an idol to worship. They are quick to share all the things they went through to boast in themselves, rather than boasting in God. We should never seek to purposely harm ourselves physically or emotionally, but we should always seek to purposely serve Christ. This alone will result in some level of persecution.

Tony Merida is one of my favorite modern expositors/commentators on the New Testament. While expounding on 2 Timothy, Merida writes, "We are most likely to suffer for the gospel when we proclaim it. While it is important to live out the gospel in deed, it is absolutely essential that we speak the gospel in word. And in speaking of the good news, we should expect opposition. We do not go looking for suffering, but we should not be surprised by it when we give verbal witness."[7]

Why should we not be surprised? For the Bible tells us so. Much of Scripture speaks to this, but this Philippians passage is often very familiar:

> Yes, and I will rejoice, for I know that through your prayers and the help of the Spirit of Jesus Christ this will turn out for my deliverance, as it is my eager expectation and hope that I will not be at all ashamed, but that with full courage now as always Christ will

---

7. Merida, *Exalting Jesus in 1 & 2 Timothy and Titus*, 152–53.

be honored in my body, whether by life or by death. For me to live is Christ, and to die is gain . . .

Only let your manner of life be worthy of the gospel of Christ, so that whether I come and see you or am absent, I may hear of you that you are standing firm in one spirit, with one mind striving side by side for the faith of the gospel, and not frightened in anything by your opponents. This is a clear sign to them of their destruction, but of your salvation, and that from God. For it has been granted to you that for the sake of Christ you should not only believe in him but also suffer for his sake, engaged in the same conflict that you saw I had and now hear that I still have. (Phil 1:18–21, 27–30)

It's right there: *for the sake of Christ you should not only believe in him but also suffer for his sake.* It is an expectation of being Christian. And because it is an expectation, we should not live in fear of it. If fact, it should be a sign of Christ's work in us. Jesus said, "Blessed are those who are persecuted for righteousness' sake, for theirs is the kingdom of heaven. Blessed are you when others revile you and persecute you and utter all kinds of evil against you falsely on my account. Rejoice and be glad, for your reward is great in heaven, for so they persecuted the prophets who were before you" (Matt. 5:10–12). As it turns out, being persecuted, for Christ's sake, is actually a sign of one's salvation.

8

Pre-Persecution in the West

Let's begin to define some terms. First, what is meant when we speak geopolitically of *the West*? When we say "the West," we are discussing Western civilization. Professor James Kurth includes the United States, Europe, Canada, Australia, and New Zealand as regions considered Western civilization. Kurth says, "Western civilization was formed from three distinct traditions: (1) the classical culture of Greece and Rome; (2) the Christian religion, particularly Western Christianity; and (3) the Enlightenment of the modern era."[1] This is in contrast to other civilizations such as Asian and Islamic civilizations. Most folks reading this book are probably from "the West."

The West is often tied directly in with our next term, *Christendom*. "Christendom" has long been understood to refer to parts of the world where most people identified themselves as Christians; these are places where cultural and regional identity is shaped by the common belief in the Bible and church history. Given Kurth's second distinction of Western civilization, it's no surprise Christendom and the West overlapped for much of the last several hundred years.

Meanwhile, *secularization*, as defined by Hunter Baker, is the "ideological position wherein religious practice and discourse must be removed from public visibility, either physically in terms of the display of religious symbols ... or rhetorically in terms of how religious ideas influence policy."[2]

---

1. Kurth, " Western Civilization."
2. Baker, "Hunter Baker on Secularism" (podcast episode).

Pre-Persecution in the West

In most of the West, secularization began during the Age of Enlightenment, largely recognized as the eighteenth century.

Kurth says, "The Enlightenment brought about the secularization of most of the intellectual elite of Christendom. This elite ensures that their civilization was no longer called that, even though much of its ordinary population remained Christian. The French Revolution and the Industrial Revolution spread Enlightenment ideas to important parts of that population, but the Christian churches continued to be a vital force within the civilization."[3] So while Western civilization and Christendom often overlap, they are no longer one in the same. Christendom, in most of the West, is over.

With the fall of Christendom came the death of *civil religion*. While Christendom generally refers to region/countries, civil religion is more about the shared values a society has pulled from that religion—things like waiting to have sex until marriage, avoiding recreational drug use, and attending church. Although these things may not have always been followed through during previous generations, there was at least a consensus opinion these were good ways to live. It is lamentable that we no longer have these shared values, but it is important to remember that none of these values should be equated with the actual gospel. In fact, Russell Moore says:

> Christian values were always more popular in American culture than the Christian gospel. That's why one could speak of "God and country" with great reception in almost any era of the nation's history but would create cultural distance as soon as one mentioned 'Christ and him crucified.' God was always welcome in American culture. He was, after all, the Deity whose job it was to bless America. The God who must be approached through the mediation of the blood of Christ, however, was much more difficult to set to patriotic music or to 'Amen' in a prayer at the Rotary Club.[4]

At one time, there was social desirability in American and other Western communities to be considered a Christian. In fact, researchers used to have to consider a "social desirability bias" around Christianity when they conducted surveys. This is "a desire on the part of the survey respondents to be perceived as more spiritually engaged than they actually are. That's because there was greater social pressure to present oneself as a person of faith—even to an anonymous interviewer."[5] Christendom

---

3. Kurth, "Western Civilization."
4. Moore, *Onward*, 6.
5. Kinnaman, and Matlock, *Faith for Exiles*, 21.

was so influential at one time that people lied about being Christian on anonymous surveys!

So while Christendom and civil religion made it easier for the Christian to live life free from persecution in the West, secularization has ultimately revealed that in America many values gleaned from Christianity (e.g., honesty, chastity, sobriety, etc.) were always more popular than the totality of the gospel message, especially the dying to oneself part.

Because we no longer have these shared values, it can no longer be assumed that people understand us when we speak of Christian ideas like salvation, grace, and forgiveness. It further complicates things now that previously shared values, especially those related to traditional teachings on sex and marriage, are not only considered unpopular, but oppressive, bigoted, and discriminatory. This matters because many of the pastors and teachers in our churches came of age in one type of society, and some of them have not adequately prepared the next generation to evangelize a very different one.

Stage 1 Persecution: Stereotyping the Targeted Group

If we remember the white-to-black gradient in the last chapter, the West finds itself in the first few pixels outside of the white area. This first stage is pretty straight forward, and you may have experienced it. If you have ever been mocked, belittled, or made fun of for being Christian, you have experienced this stage.

For example, have you ever been laughed at or have negative comments made to you while you were reading the Bible? Maybe at a lunch table or in the break room? Or maybe someone posts a meme that makes fun of all Christians. I would recommend against running around screaming or tweeting "persecution!" over a rude comment, but it certainly qualifies as stereotyping (as Professor Yancey stated). We ought to blush over the thought of claiming martyrdom at such an offense, but it does reach the barely grey level of the persecution gradient.

The stereotypes are all around us. Christians are hypocritical, judgmental, Bible-thumpers, bigoted, too political, and self-righteous. Not all Christians are like this, but many are. That's how stereotypes begin.

As unfair as it may seem, we have quite a bit of control regarding some of these stereotypes. How can we fight them? Well, let's start by not being hypocritical, judgmental, Bible-thumping, bigoted, too political, or self-righteous. Granted, that is not easy, and often times folks looking for a fight will take our words and twist them around to make us seem like any of those descriptors. In his review of *Righteous Gemstones*, an HBO satire of megachurch Christianity, Brett McCracken encourages Christians to pursue self-reflection in this area, saying, "Perhaps we should consider that the way the show depicts the [main characters]—more interested in personal comfort than costly, Christlike love; one way in church and another behind closed doors; willing to cross ethical lines in order to preserve power and influence—is actually how many people perceive evangelicals. Perhaps that's because it's closer to reality than we'd like to think."[6]

Christians have some responsibility in combatting these stereotypes. McCracken continues by explaining we can't really do much about the bias others may have towards Christians, but we are able to influence reality by "doing everything we can to live consistently Christian, honorable lives (1 Pet. 2:12) so that the raw material we give Hollywood isn't so easily satirized."

Further, we need to admit that as Christians we are all hypocrites. We have Scripture that tells us what we should and shouldn't do, and, being sinners, we will continually fall short of those expectations. This will always make us appear as hypocrites to non-believers. However, the good news is *literally* the good news! The core of the gospel is grace. Consider Paul, who in Romans 7:15–20 writes:

> For I do not understand my own actions. For I do not do what I want, but I do the very thing I hate. Now if I do what I do not want, I agree with the law, that it is good. So now it is no longer I who do it, but the sin that dwells within me. For I know that nothing good dwells in me, that is, in my flesh. For I have the desire to do what is right, but not the ability to carry it out. For I do not do the good I want, but the evil I do not want is what I keep on doing. Now if I do what I do not want, it is no longer I who do it, but sin that dwells within me.

Paul admits to being a sinner who is incapable of keeping the Law. He does what he doesn't want to do and doesn't do what he wants to do. It's sometimes hard not to be a hypocrite. However, our hypocrisy should always steer the conversations back to the main issue: we are all sinners in need of grace. As Christians, our sins need to be confessed as we seek forgiveness, but they often can also serve as a segue to preaching the gospel.

---

6. McCracken, "Righteous Gemstones."

Part 2: You Will Be Hated

No one deserves to be made fun of for being a Christian. It is likely not your fault that others say negative things towards you about Christians. However, we need to recognize that many individuals have had really, really bad experiences with church, Christians, and false Christian teachers. Often those who target someone with their anger about Christianity are really mad about some other experience. This is called misplaced anger. That being said, if you practice some of those stereotypical traits previously discussed, you may have helped create the situation you find yourself in.

We must not confuse this kind of "pre-persecution" with the more extreme examples we will see later; however, someone making fun of another person for praying is not nothing. Neither is the media mocking the Christian faith. It may be only off-white on the persecution gradient, but it's not white. We all should be facing at least this kind of pushback in our lives on occasion. If we are not living and speaking our faith outside of our comfortable church bubbles, are we really living for Christ?

Stage 2 Persecution: Vilifying the Targeted Group for Alleged Crimes or Misconduct

To vilify someone is to make him or her into "the bad guy." It's not a situation where the Christian has done anything criminal, but the persecution possibly includes *alleging* the Christian broke the law, or if nothing else, demonstrated misconduct, possibly against work or school policies. Often these allegations are really no big deal to most people when they learn what the situation is really about, but the allegations can gain momentum.

Many of the examples for stage 2 and stage 3 we are about to look at revolve around sexuality and the wedding industry. There are various issues Western society may take with orthodox Christian teaching, but these seem to be the most hotly contested in our time. Because of that, we need to pause a moment to discuss what the Bible teaches about marriage and sexual relationships for sake of consistency. The orthodox Christian view of marriage is that marriage is for one man and one woman. This definition of marriage is supported by various Bible chapters, such as Genesis 1, 2, and 19; Leviticus 19 and 20; Matthew 19; Romans 1; 1 Corinthians 6; and 1 Timothy 1, among other scriptures. As David Platt wrote, "The Bible is clear and consistent, affirming with one voice from cover to cover that homosexual activity is sexual immorality before God."[7]

7. Platt, *Counter Culture*, 170.

However, I also feel compelled to point out that the church has repeatedly failed individuals who experience same-sex attraction. We have mocked them, hated them, despised them, outed them, and then wondered why they haven't turned to Christ. We have overlooked abusive husbands, cheating spouses, fornication, and pornography, and then pearl-clutched over same-sex marriage. We say "Hate the sin and love the sinner" without understanding that many in the LGBT community see their sexuality as their identity, leaving the perception that we *do* hate them. Loving others does not include approving sin, but it does require compassion.

Scripturally, I also want to note that Paul goes as far as saying, "What business is it of mine to judge outsiders?" (1 Cor 5:12a, CSB). Meaning: take it easy when talking about sin outside of the church. We hold self-professing Christians accountable in kind, loving, and (through the local church) organized manners. When it comes to non-believers, we cannot possibly hold them to the standards God has called us to, though we are still to preach the truth. We need to be extremely gracious and patient with those outside the church, as God has been with us.

In addition, the legalization of same-sex marriage should not be viewed as the fall of United States culture and morality. While same-sex marriage is inconsistent with Scripture, there are many other things legal in our country that are inconsistent with Scripture. While the United States' founding was heavily influenced by Christian belief, ethics, and morality, we have never been a Christian theocracy. There are no laws banning pornography, adultery, or blasphemy. Gambling is legal through much of the country and there are even a few places where prostitution is as well. Legal recreational marijuana use is rapidly spreading through the states. A follower of Christ should not participate in any of this, but all of it, to some extent, is legal in the United States. If we are surrounded by sin and we choose to focus our anger towards just one group, certainly that group is going to understandably perceive we hate them.

Still, Christians are called to certain standards of behavior and may sometimes choose to separate themselves from the practice or endorsement of accepted Western behavior. Christians who do this must do so in humility and not out of anger.

One recent example involves the 2019 U.S. Women's National Soccer Team (USWNT). These women dominated the 2019 FIFA Women's World Cup, but they did so without arguably the nation's best left-back. Jaelene Hinkle (now Daniels) was a standout defender at Texas Tech, becoming

Part 2: You Will Be Hated

a starter her freshman year. Her junior year, the Red Raiders notched a team record 17 shutouts and Hinkle led the squad in assists. As a senior she earned All-American honors and was named the Big 12 Scholar Athlete of the Year. Point being: she's very, very good.

In October 2015 Hinkle, then only 22, was called up to the USWNT for her first appearance. Her international career was just taking off. Then, in June 2017, as she was preparing for friendlies (soccer term for "exhibitions") overseas against Sweden and Norway, the USWNT announced they would be wearing jerseys with the rainbow flag appearing in the numbers to promote LGBT pride. Hinkle, a Christian, did not travel with the team, and later shared, "I just felt so convicted in my spirit that it wasn't my job to wear this jersey."[8]

She did not have another call up until over a year later in July 2018, when she was invited to training camp, which angered LGBT activists. However, she did not make the team. Even a *SB Nation* blogger who called Hinkle "homophobic" admitted it was "hard to make a true soccer case for Hinkle's exclusion" from the team.[9] But as this writer points out, Hinkle was "trying to make a team that has a gay coach, several queer players, and a lot of LGBT fans." Some believe Hinkle was called to the training camp just to "provide the United States Soccer Federation with cover against any future discrimination lawsuit."[10]

Shortly after Hinkle's interview with CBN revealed her decision not to travel with the team in June 2017, her professional club team, the North Carolina Courage, took on the Portland Thorns in Portland, Oregon. Fans booed her before the game and every time she touched the ball. After the game, her coach stated, "I give her a lot of credit, to be honest. Whatever her beliefs are, whatever she believes in, that's her. It doesn't affect the team. It doesn't affect anybody on the team." A teammate echoed this sentiment, saying, "She is high on her faith, and in my honest opinion that's absolutely incredible... If she's for God, then that's fine, that's great if that's what keeps her going in her life and keeps positivity in her life, then let that be."[11]

Hinkle was left off the roster again in 2019, this time for the Women's World Cup. Because of her obedience to her Christian witness, Hinkle has been vilified by many in the soccer and sports community.

8. Root and Gill, "This Pro Soccer Player."
9. McCauley, "What on Earth."
10. Hannigan, "Religious Class."
11. *Post Wire Report*, "Soccer Player Hears Boos."

Pre-Persecution in the West

Right before I sent this book off to publication, another story along these lines arose from Louisville, Kentucky. Whitefield Academy, a Christian school, was accused of expelling a student for a picture on social media of her celebrating her birthday with a rainbow cake while wearing a rainbow sweater. Immediately, the story was portrayed as an innocent student who simply liked rainbows. If this was the entire story, the school would have clearly been in the wrong. This would be a tremendous overreaction that should have caused all Christians embarrassment. However, that was not the full story.

The school was limited in what it could share since the student was a minor. However, they did state the student had violated their code of conduct multiple times over the previous two years. In the fall of 2019 they had a meeting to give the student one last chance to follow its policies. Additionally, Rod Dreher reported the student's Instagram account included pictures of the student very clearly identifying as gay and another of her throwing her Bible into a dryer.[12]

It is beyond question that some Christians and Christian organizations have acted out of hate and fear towards those in the LGBT community. That is sinful. However, the orthodox belief on sexuality is clearly presented in Whitefield Academy's website and application materials. We can debate Bible passages, doctrine, and the best way for Christian institutions to apply these teachings. It is unfair, though, for an institution to be up front about its expectations, have parents and/or students sign off in agreement with these beliefs, and then for students who act contrary to these beliefs to portray themselves as a victim. Without investigating the case more prior to reporting on it, many in the media were complicit with vilifying Whitefield Christian Academy for simply expecting students to adhere a worldview they agreed to adhere to.

Stage 1 and stage 2 persecution are both about intimidating one's public witness. Both Hinkle and Whitefield Academy were painted as villains. Fortunately, Hinkle is able to continue playing professionally for her club team. The media fallout from the Whitefield incident is still ongoing, but as long as they followed their written policies they should not experience legal ramifications. And while I would caution Christians against vocally labeling these experiences as persecution, we can see where they fit on the persecution gradient.

---

12. Dreher, "Rainbow Cake Girl."

Part 2: You Will Be Hated

Stage 3 Persecution: Marginalizing the Targeted Group's Role in Society

Marginalization means pushing someone to the outskirts of society. It says that someone, based on his or her identity (race, gender, beliefs, etc.), does not belong in mainstream society. This marginalization in the United states is often done through accusations of crimes and/or wrongdoing that should result in the Christian or Christian group backing away from their beliefs or being prevented from engaging in parts of society.

For the Christian, we are called to do our jobs as if we are serving God (Col 3:23). If a Christian's job is to create something, they are going to do so for the glory of God. For many, turning around and selling it for a use contrary to his word is not an option. However, keep in mind that it is impossible to sell any good or service to a non-sinner. Further, if a Christian business owner chooses to not do business with a same-sex wedding or another event promoting a worldview in contradiction to his or her beliefs, that needs to be the end of it. Christians should absolutely not refuse goods and services to anyone simply because they are LGBT.

Additionally, let us keep in mind the Bible does not instruct Christians to turn down business opportunities involving same-sex weddings. This decision needs to be determined by the individual through Scripture reading, prayer, and convictions brought on by the Holy Spirit. Baking a cake for a wedding between two men is not a sin.

One of the first such stories to make national news occurred in New Mexico. In 2006, Elaine and Jonathan Huguenin, owners of Elane Photography, declined to take pictures for a "commitment ceremony" (this was before same-sex marriage was legal in New Mexico, let alone the rest of the United States). The woman who reached out to Elaine actually went on to easily find another photographer. Still, a complaint through the New Mexico Human Rights Commission was lodged. The NMHRC found against the Huguenins and ordered them to pay $6,637.94 to the couple, reimbursement for attorney's fees. The New Mexico Supreme Court upheld the decision, and in 2014 the Supreme Court of the United States declined to hear the case.[13]

Writing for *The Atlantic*, Conor Friedersdorf defended the Huguenin's religious liberty while responding to accusations labeling Elaine Huguenin as a "homophobe" and an "anti-gay bigot." Friedersdorf notes that there was

---

13. Alliance Defending Freedom, "Elane Photography"

"nothing in the public record" demonstrating that Huguenin was "afraid of gay people, or intolerant of them, or that she [bore] any hatred towards gays or lesbians."[14] Further, "The facts of her case do suggest that she regards marriage as a religious sacrament with a procreative purpose, that her Christian beliefs cause her to reject same-sex marriage, and that her business discriminates against same-sex weddings because she believes wedding photography requires artistic efforts to render the subject captured in a positive light. She believes making that effort would be wrong."

Since then, there have been many other similar cases popping up around the country related to Christians running wedding-related businesses. A bakery in Oregon. A flower shop in Washington. A boutique in Pennsylvania. They have all received varying levels of attention and government involvement. Some legal cases, such as the one involving a flower shop in Washington run by Baronnelle Stutzman, were referred back to state courts in light of the *Masterpiece Cakeshop v. Colorado Civil Rights Commission* decision.

That 2018 *Masterpiece Cakeshop* U.S. Supreme Court ruling has brought a ray of hope to many Christian business owners. In this case, a same-sex couple approached Jack Phillips to create a specially designed cake for their wedding. Phillips turned down the request based on not agreeing with the message such a cake would send. He was willing to sell any other premade cake.

The Colorado Civil Rights Commission demanded he either bake the cake with whatever message was requested or stop designing wedding cakes all together. Unlike the other cases mentioned, this one ultimately landed in front of the U.S. Supreme Court. In June of 2018, in a seven-to-two vote, the court determined the Colorado Civil Rights Commission violated Phillips's free exercise of religion by finding him in violation of the state's public accommodation law. Justice Anthony Kennedy, whom many thought would be the case's swing vote in favor of the Commission, issued a passionate majority opinion pointing out the Commission's hypocrisy:

> On at least three other occasions the Civil Rights Division considered the refusal of bakers to create cakes with images that conveyed disapproval of same-sex marriage, along with religious text. Each time, the Division found that the baker acted lawfully in refusing service. It made these determinations because, in the words of the Division, the requested cake included "wording and images [the

---

14. Friedersdorf, "Refusing to Photograph."

baker] deemed derogatory . . . A principled rationale for the difference in treatment of these two instances cannot be based on the government's own assessment of offensiveness . . . The Colorado court's attempt to account for the difference in treatment elevates one view of what is offensive over another and itself sends signal of official disapproval of Phillips' religious beliefs.[15]

Masterpiece was largely decided because the CCRC was hypocritical in enforcing the law. As Kennedy pointed out, if the law isn't being applied consistently, then the government begins to say what is and is not "offensive."

Many college students experience similar opposition on campus thanks to what are called "all-comers" policies. For colleges, the goal of such policies is to encourage inclusivity and prevent discrimination. These policies keep recognized clubs from excluding members or officeholders from adhering to certain religious beliefs. This means that at some colleges Bible-believing Christian organizations cannot actually require their officeholders to—wait for it—believe the Bible. Not being a recognized club or organization limits meeting spaces, funding, and advertising for the group. Colleges that have implemented such policies and strictly enforce them have marginalized the role of Christians on campus. Organizations such as InterVarsity and Young Life, as well as others, have faced pushback over expectations of its student leaders to adhere to certain doctrine.

One final example of marginalization comes from Canada, where "leading Canadian and British bioethicists argue" that "authorities should bar doctors from refusing to provide such services as abortion and assisted suicide on moral grounds, *and screen out potential medical students* who might impose their values on patients."[16] What they are arguing is this: if a doctor objects to doing abortion him or herself, or helping a patient kill him or herself, that person should not be permitted to be a doctor. This isn't simply about something being legal or not; it's about not even allowing room for a debate on the morality of abortion or assisted suicide. Doing this would effectively bar Christians from being doctors. Albert Mohler comments on this story:

> We're seeing the constricting of the culture in so many ways, the closing of so many doors to those who are confessionally and convictionally Christian. And we are seeing this across the professions, first and foremost because the licensure of those who hold

---

15. French, "In *Masterpiece Cakeshop*."
16. Blackwell, "Ban Conscientious Objection," Emphasis added.

this kind of professional status, either a license to practice law or a license to practice medicine, similar kinds of licensure, this is where immediately a regulatory society can begin coercively to enforce this kind of moral revolution.

He continues:

> In recent decades, Canada has been markedly more secular than the 50 American states to the south. But one of the most interesting trends of recent years is that the United States has been catching up with Canada on the score. It will not be safe, nor would it be honest, for Christians in the United States to say that this is a debate that is safely across our northern border. On issue after issue in the moral revolution, the United States has followed Canada in terms of adopting many of these very same secular moral proposals. With the acceleration of this moral revolution, you should expect this kind of argument to show up on this side of the border in very short order.[17]

Stage 3 persecution is about marginalizing Christians for their beliefs and excluding their voices in the public sphere. Those who express unpopular aspects of the Christian faith have had their businesses fined and closed down. They have been derecognized as college organizations and forced to meet off campus. It's not about preventing Christians from being in public, but about preventing the practice or espousal of unpopular aspects of Christianity in public.

Recall our discussion of secularism. Hunter Baker also defined secularism more succinctly as "religious considerations [being] excluded from civil affairs." Some may counter with, "Separation of church and state!," but they are not one in the same. Baker argues, "Secularism is not and should not be synonymous with the separation of church and state. The separation of church and state, in the classical sense, simply means that the state does not collect fees to support the church; neither does it mandate membership in the church."[18] Stage 3 persecution is about using social and legal pressure to compel Christians to keep their faith to themselves when in public, not merely keeping it out of government.

Fortunately court decisions such as the aforementioned U.S. Supreme Court's 2018 decision on *Masterpiece Cakeshop v. Colorado Civil Rights Commission*, the Eighth Circuit Court of appeals decision on *Telescope*

---

17. Mohler, *The Briefing* (podcast), September 28, 2016.
18. Baker, *End of Secularism*, 19.

Part 2: You Will Be Hated

Media Group v. Lucero and Ellison, a U.S. District Court's decision in *InterVarsity Christian Fellowship v. University of Iowa*, a U.S. District Court's decision in *Buck v. Gordon*, and the Arizona Supreme Court's decision on *Brush & Nib Studio v. City of Phoenix* have created at least a reprieve from some of this coercion. Though, more recently, it's worth mentioning the "enthusiastic response"[19] a CNN town hall gave to a presidential candidate who quickly affirmed his desire to remove tax-exempt status from churches and Christians college that do not conform to worldly views regarding marriage and gender.

Christians need to be careful about how they portray these early stages of persecution. The stories shared in this chapter are more about understanding the increasing unpopularity of Christian teaching in the West than any faux martyrdom. My goal is to highlight the increasing unpopularity of Christian teaching in the West. For much of the Western world, such objection to Christian teaching and aversion to Christian practice are necessary for a modern society. We won't change many hearts for Christ if we spend too much of our time justifying why we do not want to do business with those we disagree with.

We also need to admit that what we call "persecution" in the West pales in comparison to what our brothers and sisters in Christ face in many other regions of the world. The enmity some Christians face in the West may make us feel uncomfortable or marginalized, but what Christians in China, Pakistan, and Iran face is deadly.

---

19. Inazu, "Democrats Are Going to Regret."

9

Persecution Around the World

In the last chapter we examined the various ways persecution plays out in the Western world. Such persecution is real, and it should not be ignored. It may be subtle or pretty pale on our gradient, but it's not nothing. However, what we face in the United States and elsewhere in the West is significantly insignificant compared to what our brothers and sisters in Christ face in other parts of the world.

Voice of the Martyrs (VOM) "is a nonprofit, interdenominational missions organization that offers practical and spiritual help to persecuted Christians around the world."[1] It was founded in 1967 by Richard Wurmbrand, himself a pastor who was imprisoned for 14 years in Communist Romania. This topic is VOM's area of expertise.

VOM identifies countries that are monitored ("a trend towards increased persecution of Christians"), hostile ("nations where governments consistently attempt to provide protection for the Christian population but Christians are routinely persecuted by family, friends, neighbors or political groups"), and restricted ("countries where government-sanctioned circumstances or anti-Christian laws lead to Christians being harassed, imprisoned, killed or deprived of possessions or liberties").[2]

As of 2019, restricted countries include nations like China, Cuba, Egypt, Iraq, Jordan, Libya, Morocco, Pakistan, Qatar, Saudi Arabia, and many others. Many of these countries receive foreign aid from the United States. China is one of five permanent members of the United Nations Security Council

---

1. Voice of the Martyrs, "About VOM."
2. Voice of the Martyrs, *2019 Global Prayer Guide*.

Part 2: You Will Be Hated

(thereby giving them veto power). Qatar is hosting the 2022 FIFA World Cup. Egypt, Pakistan, Saudi Arabia, and others are considered U.S. allies. Point being: it's not just ISIS out there trying to subdue Christianity.

Voice of the Martyrs has a lot of great ways to get involved in their ministry, including praying, donating money, and writing letters to those imprisoned. Many of those they work with in the fields of these countries will never be known to you or me, but God knows their labor, and we must not forget them in our prayers. You can call them brave, but I venture to imagine they would rather be called obedient. One anonymous missionary in Myanmar said, "I would be very happy to get persecuted, if only the Lord counts me as worthy."

This echoes Acts 5. The early Christian church was off to a great start. After Jesus ascended to heaven, the disciples returned to Jerusalem and voted in a new member. Then the Holy Spirit descended, Peter preached a bold sermon, lame were healed, and more came to believe in Jesus. Despite being arrested and brought before the council, Peter and John were able to depart with no ill treatment. Shortly later the believers were jailed again, though they would be released by an angel and sent back to the temple to continue preaching.

At his wit's end, the high priest again ordered them to cease preaching the name of Jesus. The believers responded:

> We must obey God rather than men. The God of our fathers raised Jesus, whom you killed by hanging him on a tree. God exalted him at his right hand as Lord and Savior, to give repentance to Israel and forgiveness of sins. And we are witnesses to these things, and so is the Holy Spirit whom God has given to those who obey him. (Acts 5:29b–32)

Although the enraged council wanted to kill them, a Pharisee named Gamaliel calmed them down, and the believers were "only" beaten before being released. Luke writes, "Then they left the presence of the council, *rejoicing that they were counted worthy to suffer dishonor for the name*" (Acts 5:41, emphasis added). The believers did not halt their preaching.

We also learn from Peter, who tells us:

> Beloved, do not be surprised at the fiery trial when it comes upon you to test you, as though something strange were happening to you. But rejoice insofar as you share Christ's sufferings, that you may also rejoice and be glad when his glory is revealed. If you are insulted for the name of Christ, you are blessed, because the Spirit

of glory and of God rests upon you. But let none of you suffer as a murderer or a thief or an evildoer or as a meddler. Yet if anyone suffers as a Christian, let him not be ashamed, but let him glorify God in that name . . . Therefore let those who suffer according to God's will entrust their souls to a faithful Creator while doing good. (1 Pet 4:12–16, 19)

This frontline worker in Myanmar, and those whose stories we are about to read, have entrusted their souls to a "faithful Creator." They count severe suffering as a blessing. And if that is the case, they should feel especially blessed, for their suffering is great.

Stage 4 Persecution: Criminalizing the Targeted Group or Its Work

In earlier stages, the persecution takes the form of intimidation, allegation, and marginalization. The mechanisms of this very mild persecution are ostracizing or using the law as it is written (i.e., not a law intended to punish Christians) to target and penalize Christians. Stage 4, however, is about making Christian practices illegal. These could be restrictions on anything from public prayer to evangelism. Frequently it includes anti-blasphemy laws.

Anti-blasphemy laws are those that restrict what citizens can say against or in contradiction of the state-sanctioned religion. State-sanctioned religions are theocracies. Theocracies are on the other side of the spectrum from secularism. If secularism is the complete removal of religion from the public square, theocracies are the complete melding together of government and religion. Considering theocracies tend to be in Muslim countries, it still results in the same for Christians: keep your faith to yourself.

In the U.S. State Department's 2015 *International Religious Freedom Report,* it states that anti-blasphemy laws "conflict with and undermine universally recognized human rights."[3] Those basic human rights include speech and religion. But not only do they deny those rights, they often encourage rogue, vigilante "justice" against the offender of such a law.

Writing for *The Washington Post,* Carol Morello noted after reading this report:

> Iran executed 20 people last year for "enmity against God." Saudi Arabia penalizes blasphemy with lengthy prison sentences and

---

3. Bureau of Democracy, *International Religious Freedom Report.*

Part 2: You Will Be Hated

lashings. In Nigeria, a sharia court sentenced nine people to death for elevating their sect's founder over the prophet Muhammed. In Afghanistan, a woman falsely accused of burning a Koran was stoned and burned alive by an angry mob. A 7-year-old Syrian boy in the area ruled by the Islamic State was killed by firing squad after he cursed God during a soccer game. Mobs have killed more than 60 people since 1990 for crimes such as desecrating the Koran or insulting the prophet.[4]

Say what you will about angry, bitter, and judgmental fundamentalist Christians, but I cannot name a single time they executed a first-grader for taking the Lord's name in vain.

One well-known case of stage 4 persecution involves a woman named Asia Bibi. Bibi was a Christian in Pakistan arrested by police on June 19, 2009. She was charged with blasphemy as a result of an intense conversation about faith with other women, all Muslim. Bibi was pressured to renounce her faith, but responded, "Our Christ sacrificed his life on the cross for our sins . . . Our Christ is alive." Bibi was then beaten and locked in a room, and it was "announced from mosque loudspeakers that she would be punished by having her face blackened and being paraded through the village on a donkey." Christians in the area contacted the police, who initially took her into custody for her protection. However, the police were pressured to file the blasphemy charges.[5]

On November 8, 2010, Bibi was sentenced to death and was given seven days to appeal. The appeal was filed, but multiple individuals in the government who had expressed support for Bibi were assassinated. One appeal, scheduled for October 13, 2016, was cancelled when the judge refused to participate. His objection was based on having been a part of one of the cases involving an assassinated government official, which supposedly created a conflict. However, it is widely understood that the judge felt he was in a no-win situation. This judge must have known it was wrong to have Bibi executed, but also knew to prevent it would be to bring death upon himself.

On October 31, 2018, Bibi was acquitted of the charge, but on November 2, 2018, the government barred her from leaving Pakistan, leaving her open for potential vigilante "justice." Finally, on January 29, 2019, Bibi's acquittal was upheld and she was free to leave the country. While she arrived safely in Canada, "Islamic extremists have pledged to pursue the Christian

---

4. Morello, "State Department."
5. Voice of the Martyrs, "Prisoner Profile."

woman and kill her for the act of blasphemy . . . Bibi may spend the rest of her days looking over her should in fear of an international assassin."[6]

Asia Bibi is far from being alone when it comes to being jailed for espousing the Christian faith. Saaed Abedini is an Iranian-American pastor who was successful with the home church movement in Iran in the early 2000s after converting from Islam to Christianity early in his teenage years.

In 2005, Mahmoud Ahmadinejad was elected president of Iran, and with him came great suppression of such home churches. As a result, Abedini and his wife returned to the United States. He would make numerous trips back and forth between the U.S. and Iran until 2012, when the Islamic Revolutionary Guard Corps confiscated his passport and placed him under arrest. Eventually, it was announced that Abedini was being charged with undermining "the Iranian government by creating a network of Christian house churches and that he was attempting to sway Iranian youth away from Islam."[7] Abedini was sent to Rajai Shahr, a notorious Iranian prison, "regarded as one of Iran's harshest jails because of its many reported cases of torture, rape and murder."[8] Finally, in January of 2016, after international pressure from Amnesty International and the United States government, including U.S. President Barack Obama and Secretary of State John Kerry, Abedini was released.

Beyond Iran's northwest border, on July 15, 2016, an attempted coup was undertaken in Turkey. The Turkish government managed to hold on to power, but since has commenced cracking down on anyone they suspect associated with the attempt. Americans ministering in the area were deemed "national threats" and either banned and deported or jailed. One pastor, Andrew Brunson, who had had been ministering in the region for over 20 years, was arrested on October 7 of that year, being searched and having his phone confiscated. Then, "Instead of being deported he was held with no charges for 63 days, during which time he was denied access to his Turkish attorney." He spent time in solitary confinement "with his glasses and watch confiscated."[9]

Things grew worse on December 8, when in the middle of the night he was transported to a counterterrorism unit. There, "He was questioned and [was] falsely charged with 'membership in an armed terrorist organization.'

6. Sherwood, "Asia Bibi."
7. Kellog, "Iran Sentences American Pastor."
8. Greenslade, "Iran Jails Women Journalists."
9. Sekulow, "American Pastor Andrew Brunson."

The charging documents state no 'evidence has been gathered' against him. A Turkish judge had the option to deport Pastor Andrew, release him on weekly sign-ins at the local police station, or imprison him. The judge chose to remand Pastor Andrew to prison."[10]

Fortunately, on October 12, 2018 (just over two years from his initial captivity), under pressure from U.S. President Donald Trump and Vice President Mike Pence, Brunson was freed. Turkey, long an example of stability in a hostile region, is steadily increasing undue restriction of Christian practice. Family of a good friend of mine, who were living and ministering in Turkey for years, recently fled out of fear that they would face a plight similar to Brunson's. For the safety of Americans they know in Turkey, I can't elaborate, but all members of their family are safe back in the United States.

While American Christians face various degrees of pressure in the public sphere, our brothers and sisters abroad are being jailed and face severe penalties as a result of vague claims of blasphemy and security. However, as we already know, there is one final stage of persecution.

Stage 5 Persecution: Persecuting the Targeted Group Outright

The final stage is the darkest section of our persecution gradient. Here, we are speaking of blatant and outright persecution of Christians. This is not simply laws against evangelism or public prayer, but actively seeking out and attempting to end Christianity and Christian influence in a region. Two notable examples arise from China and the Middle East.

Things were never great between the Chinese government and Christianity, but relations took a dark turn in 2016. Congyi Church was the largest Christian church in China, able to host 5,500 worshippers when it completed its building in 2005. Eventually the congregation even outgrew this space. On January 29, 2016, the church's pastor, Gu Yuese, who had become "the highest-ranking church official sanctioned by the Chinese Community Party," was arrested for allegedly embezzling $1.6 million, though it's unclear where that money would have come from (try to find a rich Christian congregation in China) and no evidence has been produced.[11]

10. Sekulow, "American Pastor Andrew Brunson."
11. Hong, "China's Crackdown."

Only a couple months later, government officials undertook a great campaign to demolish or at least cause destruction to numerous church buildings in China. *The Christian Post* reported in March of 2016, "Groups of hundreds Chinese officers sent by the Communist Party demolished over a dozen church crosses in China's coastal Zhejiang province this past week, leading to confrontations with protesters, some of whom were beaten and bloodied."[12]

Not all protestors were "only" beaten and bloodied, however. The next month, "A Christian house church leader and his wife were buried alive in China's central Henan province for protesting against the government-ordered demolition of their church, and while the man managed to escape, his wife suffocated to death."[13]

While many churches in this region of China were left standing, they were not left untouched. Writing for *The New York Times*, Ian Johnson described the standing churches in the Zhejiang Province as "decapitated" due to the removal of the crosses standing atop church steeples. Government officials used blowtorches and saws to take down the most recognized physical symbol of the Christian faith.[14]

More recently, Pastor Wang Yi of Rain Covenant Church was sentenced to nine years in prison. This was not simply for leading an unregistered house church, but for allegedly distributing Christian materials without government approval. Additionally, he "ran an unapproved school and seminary through the church."[15] Yi is especially high-profile since he visited the White House in 2006.

Many activists are calling this recent crackdown, "the worst . . . on religion since the country's Cultural Revolution, when Mao Zedong's government vowed to eradicate religion."[16] Additionally, part of the Chinese government's plan to run the Christian church in its country is to retranslate and annotate "the Bible, to find commonalities with socialism and establish a 'correct understanding' of the text."

To be clear, it's not just Christians China has targeted. In fact, Muslims have it even worse. "Since 2017, over 1 million Uyghur Muslims have been forced into mass interment—and in some cases labor camps—where

12. Zaimov, "Hundreds of Police."
13. Zaimov, "Church Leader's Wife."
14. Johnson, "Decapitated Churches."
15. Kidd, "China Sentences Pastor Wang Yi."
16. Kuo, "In China, They're Closing Churches."

Part 2: You Will Be Hated

they're forced to undergo brutal Chinese reeducation sessions."[17] China's fear of religion runs deep.

While the Chinese government does not accept the gospel, they evidently understand how powerful it is. China is a communist country. Communism by definition needs the government as all-powerful, requiring complete obedience from its citizens. China's government cannot maintain power over its citizens if Christianity continues to spread. Not because of a violent Christian rebellion against the government, but because once someone has committed his or her life to Christ, any submission to human authority becomes secondary. While Scripture compels us to obey government, as we previously discussed, it gives the caveat to ignore government when it coerces us to do something counter to God's commands.

The Australian Broadcasting Company reports that there is "good reason to why the Communist Party is threatened by the Church. Some say there are 100 million Christians in China—that's more than the Communist Party members."[18] Some reports even estimate that by 2030 China could be home to the world's largest Christian population. A communist regime with tens and potentially hundreds of millions of citizens refusing to kneel to government coercion against their faith will not tolerate the expansion of Christianity.

Another well-known example of stage 5 persecution brings us to the Middle East and the horrifying actions of ISIS. ISIS stands for the Islamic State of Iraq and Syria. Sometimes it's referred to as ISIL, abbreviating the Islamic State of Iraq and the Levant. Sometimes they are simply referred to as the Islamic State.

ISIS was an Islamic militant group connected with Al-Qaeda in 2004, but later broke apart due to "differences in doctrine and objectives." The end goal for ISIS "is to establish a caliphate to rule over the entire Muslim world, under a single leader and in line with Sharia (Islamic law)."[19] The root word in "caliphate" is *caliph*, which is one who is believed to be a successor to Muhammed. [20]

For this global caliphate to take place, *jihad* is necessary. There are many opinions on what "jihad" means in practice, but the word translates as *struggle*. Some take this to mean an internal struggle with one's Muslim

---

17. Nardi, "Xi Jinping Ramps Up Religious Persecution," *National Review*
18. Carney, "Chinese Communist Party."
19. Carter, "9 Things You Should Know."
20. Chandler, "What Is an Islamic Caliphate?"

Persecution Around the World

faith, others as a struggle to build a Muslim society, yet still it can also be used to refer to a holy war. For ISIS, this struggle includes claiming land in the Middle East, and then expanding their territory.

To fully understand the conflicts in the Middle East, one will need to do extensive research on religion, history, politics, and current events. My goal here is not to even pretend I am qualified to do that. I only want to establish a very, very basic point of reference when discussing some of ISIS's actions.

In July 2014, ISIS appeared on the radar of Americans when they gave Christians in Mosul, Iraq the choice to convert to Islam, pay a tax, leave, or die. For many, the only choice was to flee, leaving behind everything but their lives and the clothes on their back. At this time, "all 30 churches and monasteries in the city" went under ISIS control. Crosses were "removed from all of them" with some of them being "burned, destroyed, and looted."[21]

A few months later, in February of 2015, the Western world woke up to images of 21 men clad in orange jumpsuits being paraded on a beach in Libya. These men were Coptic Christians, a sect of orthodox Christians who trace their history to first century Egypt. These men were forced to kneel, with members of ISIS behind them dressed in black. The Coptic Christians were then beheaded. The release of the video was part of ISIS propaganda.[22] The scene was repeated again that April with two separate groups of Ethiopian Christians, half beheaded on a beach along the Mediterranean Sea, and the others shot in southern Libya.[23]

In December of 2016, ISIS took credit for attacking a Sunday morning Mass in Cairo, Egypt, another attack on Coptic Christians. "A bomb ripped through the chapel in the cathedral complex... killing 25 people and wounding another 49, mostly women and children." It was called "one of the deadliest attacks on the country's Christian minority in recent memory."[24]

ISIS has claimed responsibility for attacks around the world which have resulted in thousands of victims dead or injured. Many of their attacks have been directed at Christian gatherings. They attacked a mass in France in 2016, two Palm Sunday services in Egypt in 2017, a Russian Orthodox church in 2018, and bombed three churches in Indonesia in 2018. In 2019,

---

21. Carter, "FAQs."
22. "ISIS Video."
23. McLaughlin, "ISIS Executes More Christians."
24. Fam and Hendawi, "Bomb Kills 25."

253 individuals were killed on Easter in Sri Lanka and 10 Christian hostages in Nigeria were executed on Christmas day.

What our brothers and sisters in Christ are facing in areas like Syria, Iraq, Egypt, and elsewhere in the Middle East is the darkest section of our persecution gradient. These followers of Christ are being kidnapped, beheaded, and bombed, with the Islamic State hoping to blot out Christian existence from history. While persecution is a gradient and goes in stages, this is what our minds, our hearts, and our prayers should rest on when we consider the term.

Most of us will never face this kind of persecution, but we cannot forget about our brothers and sisters who do. Their ministries come at great cost. They speak the name of Jesus, the same name we are called to speak. We are connected to them in faith and will one day meet them in eternity. We must remember them in our prayers and draw from their courage in whatever uncomfortable positions we may find ourselves in.

And yet—and this is going to seem calloused—there is a worse attack on the Christian faith than what the Islamic State could ever do. You see, as a Christian, we believe in eternity. We believe in a heaven. One day Jesus will separate his followers from those who did not know him (Matt 25:32). We believe that Jesus is the only way to heaven (John 14:6), therefore anything that takes one away from Jesus leads to eternal damnation (Matt 13: 40–43; Rev 20:15). If this is what we believe—if we honestly say that Jesus is the only way to heaven—then there must be something worse that the Islamic State beheading believing Christians. There must be something worse than a physical death. That something is anything leading people away from Jesus, including false Christian teaching. And while I believe the evil in an ISIS militant's heart is far darker than that of a false teacher, the end result of being led away from Christ is worse.

10

Persecution from False Teaching

It might seem radical to imply twisting Scripture or abusing doctrine is even remotely comparable to the persecution Christians are facing in the Middle East. Trust me when I say it makes me wince too. Before you write me or the rest of this book off, we need to revisit Matthew 24:3–14 with a couple lines italicized for emphasis:

> As he sat on the Mount of Olives, the disciples came to him privately, saying, "Tell us when will these things be, and what will be the sign of your coming and of the end of the age?" And Jesus answered them, *"See that no one leads you astray. For many will come in my name, saying, 'I am the Christ,' and they will lead many astray.* And you will hear of wars and rumors of wars. See that you are not alarmed, for this must take place, but the end is not yet. For nation will rise against nation, and kingdom against kingdom, and there will be famines and earthquakes in various places. All these are but the beginning of the birth pains.
>
> "Then they will deliver you up to tribulation and put you do death, and you will be hated by all nations for my name's sake. And then many will fall away and betray one another and hate one another. *And many false prophets will arise and lead many astray.* And because lawlessness will be increased, the love of many will grow cold. *But the one who endures to the end will be saved.* And this gospel of the kingdom will be proclaimed throughout the whole world as a testimony to all nations, and then the end will come." (emphasis added)

Amidst Jesus' warnings regarding people hating his followers for their faith is a second warning: false prophets will lead many astray; that is, they will take individuals professing faith in Christ by the hand, whisper deceitful messages, and escort them from the foot of the cross towards something that cannot save their souls, be it wealth, works, peace, or something else. The blade of an Islamic militant can sever the head, but it cannot destroy the soul.

Warnings against false teachers saturate the pages of New Testament. Here are just a few more examples:

Jesus:

> Beware of false prophets, who come to you in sheep's clothing but inwardly are ravenous wolves. You will recognize them by their fruits. Are grapes gathered from thornbushes, or figs from thistles? So, every healthy tree bears good fruit, but the diseased tree bears bad fruit. A healthy tree cannot bear bad fruit, nor can a diseased tree bear good fruit. Every tree that does not bear good fruit is cut down and thrown into the fire. Thus you will recognize them by their fruits. (Matt 7:15–17)

Paul:

> I appeal to you, brothers, to watch out for those who cause divisions and create obstacles contrary to the doctrine that you have been taught; avoid them. For such persons do not serve our Lord Christ, but their own appetites, and by smooth talk and flattery they deceive the hears of the naïve. (Rom 16:17–18)

> And what I am doing I will continue to do, in order to undermine the claim of those who would like to claim that in their boasted mission they work on the same terms as we do. For such men are false apostles, deceitful workmen, disguising themselves as apostles of Christ. And no wonder, for even Satan disguises himself as an angel of light. So it is no surprise if his servants, also, disguise themselves as servants of righteousness. Their end will correspond to their deeds. (2 Cor 11:12–15)

> For the time is coming when people will not endure sound teaching, but having itching ears they will accumulate for themselves teachers to suit their own passions, and will turn away from listening to the truth and wander off into myths. As for you, always be sober-minded, endure suffering, do the work of an evangelist, fulfill your ministry. (2 Tim 4:3–4)

John:

Persecution from False Teaching

> Beloved, do not believe every spirit, but test the spirits to see whether they are from God, for many false prophets have gone out into the world. By this you know the Spirit of God: every spirit that confesses that Jesus Christ has come in the flesh is from God, and every spirit that does not confess Jesus is not from God. This is the spirit of the antichrist, which you heard was coming and now is in the world already. (1 John 4:1–3)

False teachers lead astray. They are ravenous wolves. They create obstacles contrary to doctrine. They are deceitful workmen. They promote myths. They are led by spirits who do not confess Jesus as savior. Scripture consistently warns against those who will come before us, allegedly in the name of God, and point to something other than Jesus. False teaching is as alive today as it ever was in the church's history, and too many young adult Christians are swept up in this deceit because they were never even warned, let alone taught how to recognize it. We *cannot* be silent in the face of false teaching. False teaching is Satan's persecution on the church.

This especially matters for young adults. Certainly some have been raised in churches that bad-mouthed other churches. But that's not the same as teaching discernment and recognizing unbiblical teaching. Many young adult Christians have not been prepared to identify, let alone counter, false teaching.

How Will We know?

In Matthew 7, quoted above, Jesus explains that we will know false teachers by their fruit. That's obviously true, but it does not mean it's easy. Tim Challies offers seven marks of a false teacher:

1. False teachers are man pleasers.
2. False teachers save their harshest criticism for God's most faithful servants.
3. False teachers teach their own wisdom and vision.
4. False teachers miss what is of central importance and focus instead on the small details.
5. False teachers obscure their false doctrine behind eloquent speech and what appears to be impressive logic.

6. False teachers are more concerned with winning others to their opinions than in helping and bettering them.

7. False teachers exploit their followers.[1]

As you read through this list, note a reoccurring trait: there is more concern about the horizontal than the vertical. These teachers try to impress other men, they rely on man's logic, they are concerned about man's opinion, and they look to create influence over fellow men. Instead, a teacher of the true gospel should concern himself with things that are vertical—things that are of God. They seek to be faithful to God, convey God's teaching, point others to God, and are concerned about what God says.

Challies explains, "no one enriches hell more than false teachers. No one finds greater joy in drawing people away from truth and leading them into error. False teachers have been present in every era of human history, they have always been a plague and have always been in the business of providing counterfeit truth."[2]

We must have a critical eye and ear to what is being taught. This does not mean we treat everyone with skepticism and mistrust. We evaluate teaching by holding it up against Scripture. Sometimes incorrect teaching may be the ravenous wolf; other times it could be a confused Apollos not fully understanding the gospel and needing Priscilla and Aquila's gentle and loving corrections (Acts 18:24–27).

It is also important to understand there are different types of disagreements we may have in the church. I have heard a distinction described as closed-hand issues versus open-hand issues. The closed-hand issues we need to be firm on: things like Jesus being the only way to heaven, Jesus existing as fully God and fully man, and salvation by grace through faith. Disagreement on these topics are deal-breakers and we cannot accept unorthodoxy in these areas.

However, other important, but less clear disagreements may arise and we must hold those matters in an open hand. These may be issues that cause us to worship differently or in different congregations, but they should not result in any accusations of heresy. I would place the predestination–free will debate in this category. Christians (legally) drinking alcohol in moderation is another one. As is the method and timing of baptism. Even the complementarian-egalitarian debate is a non-essential

1. Challies, "7 Marks of a False Teacher."
2. Challies, "7 Marks of a False Teacher."

issue. If we hold on tight to the more important matters, then these lesser ones do not require disunity.

This is reminiscent of an old Lutheran saying: *In necessariis unitas, in dublis libertas, in omnibus caritas.* It translates as: In essentials unity, in non-essentials liberty, in all things charity. What it means is there are essential issues like who Jesus is and how to obtain salvation. There are other non-essential issues which we have the liberty to disagree on. But ultimately, we approach both situations with *caritas*—Christian love.

This means essential issues matter and we need to be unified on them. We need to be prepared to recognize when essential issues are taught wrongly. Let's practice.

Three Examples of Prosperity Gospel False Teaching

The prosperity gospel is an especially widespread false teaching in the United States. In the U.S., we cherish our freedoms, our individuality, and our ability to better our lives through the free market. None of this is necessarily bad. However, when we add it to the Christian faith, it's incredibly dangerous. At its core, the prosperity gospel (also known as the health and wealth gospel) teaches Christians will receive more blessings from God as they increase their faith. These teachers need to read chapter 6 of this book!

Below you will find three quotes from three different prominent prosperity gospel teachers. After you read the first one, set the book down and contemplate whether this sounds like something of Scripture. If it sounds contradictory to something you have read in your Bible, try to locate the passage. Do this for each of the three quotes.

> Quote 1: "When you focus on being a blessing, God makes sure that you are always blessed in abundance."[3]

> Quote 2: "God will not move unless I say it. Why? Because He has made us coworkers with him. He set things up that way."[4]

> Quote 3: "Anyone who tells you to deny yourself is from Satan."[5]

Let's start with quote 1. This teacher is saying your focus should prioritize being a blessing, and that in return God will make sure you are

---

3. Osteen, *Your Best Life Now*, 225.
4. Hinn, *Anointing*, 81.
5. Horton, "Evangelicals Should Be Deeply Troubled."

Part 2: You Will Be Hated

always in abundance. Chiefly, this teacher is portraying God's relationship with us as a *quid pro quo*—a Latin phrase meaning that if you do a favor for someone, you get something in return.

Testing this against Scripture, I see at least three major issues. First, recommending your focus be on being a blessing implies that the focus *should not* be on Jesus. Think of a camera. When you focus in on one subject, everything else gets a little blurry. That does not mean you don't care about everything else in the frame, but it becomes a background. For Christians, the focus should always be Jesus. Colossians 3:2 tells us to "set [our] minds on things that are above."

My second issue is this quote teaches that if you do x you will get y. That's a vending machine, not God. Read a fraction of Paul's writings and you'll know that whatever we receive is based on God's grace and not our works (Rom 9:16; Gal 2:21; and Eph 2:8–9 just to name a few).

Third, it suggests that by being faithful your reward is earthly abundance, discounting the splendor and magnanimity of salvation. Paul writes in Philippians 3:7–8, "But whatever gain I had, I counted as loss for the sake of Christ. Indeed, I count everything as loss because of the surpassing worth of knowing Christ Jesus my Lord. For his sake I have suffered the loss of all things and count them as rubbish, in order that I may gain Christ." Being a Christian isn't about getting "blessed in abundance." Paul's example is that of a man who would lose everything in this world to gain Christ. That is not to say it is evil to drive a Tesla, own a big house, and climb the corporate ladder. What it does mean is that all of those things are meaningless at the foot of the cross.

In quote 2 we are presented with this idea that God will not act until we say so. The reason? God has made us equals with him. Um, no, he hasn't.

You are not equal with God. We may have been made coheirs with Christ (Rom 8:17), but that does not mean we are equal. Psalm 135:6 says, "Whatever the Lord pleases, he does" (NASB). Christian, I can't make it much simpler than that. God is sovereign and you are not. King Nebuchadnezzar learned this the hard way. In Daniel 4 we read of how Nebuchadnezzar mocked God by declaring his own greatness over Babylon. The Lord sent the king to the fields, where he remained eating grass like an ox with his hair and fingernails growing to gross lengths. Eventually, returned to his senses, Nebuchadnezzar declared God's "dominion is an everlasting dominion, and his kingdom endures from generation to generation; all the inhabitants of the earth are accounting as nothing, and he does according to his will among the

Persecution from False Teaching

host of heaven and among the inhabitants of the earth; and none can stay his hand or say to him, 'What have you done?'" (Dan 4:34–35).

All of this to say God *will move* whether you say so or not. My experience is that God's will *will* be done with or without your involvement; therefore, you may as well join up on the winning team.

The third quote is from another popular Christian teacher. Read this quote again: "Anyone who tells you to deny yourself is from Satan." Please tell me your false teaching alarm is going bonkers! If you have been a Christian for more than a few days, hopefully the "deny yourself" part is reverberating in your mind. Doesn't that sound familiar to you? It should. Jesus taught his disciples:

> And he said to all, "If anyone would come after me, *let him deny himself* and take up his cross daily and follow me. For whoever would save his life will lose it, but whoever loses his life for my sake will save it. For what does it profit a man if he gains the whole world and loses or forfeits himself?" (Luke 9:23–25, emphasis added)

The speaker of quote 3 says that anyone who tells you to deny yourself is from Satan. Meanwhile, Jesus *literally* tells his followers to deny themselves. I don't believe this teacher is purposefully trying to say Jesus is Satan, however, that is ultimately what happens when taking this false teaching at face value. The teacher just wants to encourage you and make you feel better about yourself. Alone, that's not a problem. When the advice is directly counter to the words of Jesus, it is a *huge* problem. And, as an aside, in 2019 this individual was granted an influential role in the White House.

In all three of these quotes, we see essential doctrine violated. Grace, God's sovereignty, and denying ourselves and submitting God (Gal 2:20) are all basic fundamental issues for the Christian. We must agree on them. Yet these three teachers, all of whom have extensive followings, contradict them.

As a Christian, you need to be prepared to hold firm against this kind of teaching and to be able to recognize it when you hear it. How can you ready yourself? Study Scripture. I am not the best example of someone who has committed himself to studying the Bible as much as he can. I have a lot of room for improvement. But I have spent enough time reading to recall Scripture that alerts me these kind of errors. Let's revisit:

> Quote 1 says: "When you focus on being a blessing, God makes sure that you are always blessed in abundance."
>
> Scripture says: "But whatever gain I had, I counted as loss for the sake of Christ. Indeed, I count everything as loss because of the

surpassing worth of knowing Christ Jesus my Lord. For his sake I have suffered the loss of all things and count them as rubbish, in order that I may gain Christ" (Phil 3:7–8).

Quote 2 says: "God will not move unless I say it. Why? Because He has made us coworkers with Him. He set things up that way."

Scripture says: "Whatever the Lord pleases, he does" (Ps 135:6, NASB).

Quote 3 says: "Anyone who tells you to deny yourself is from Satan."

Scripture says: "If anyone would come after me, let him deny himself and take up his cross daily and follow me" (Luke 9:23).

The first time I read each of these quotes, I was immediately able to recall Scripture somewhere countering them. I might not have been able to flip to the exact passage right away, but I knew enough to hit the pause button and examine God's Word. The more you and I spend studying Scripture, the better we will be able to prevent this form of persecution from taking root in our lives and in our churches.

And it is persecution. Remember, we used this definition for persecution: "to harass or punish in a manner designed to injure, grieve, or afflict; *specifically*: to cause to suffer because of belief." Whereas the kinds of persecution we previously outlined tend to be tangible, the persecution that comes from false teaching is more abstract. However, there is teaching labeled as Christian that actually draws you away from Jesus; it is injurious to your faith, and you may even eternally suffer from it. Remember, Jesus tells us that many will rise who will attempt to lead us astray. We must endure to the end.

And we need to be willing to check our own beliefs from time to time. Brett McCracken writes, "We may not go so far as to assume faith will lead us to health and wealth, but many of us still approach faith primarily through a 'what does it do for me?' consumerist lens."[6] Do we look for the church with the music that gives us just the right emotional high? Must we decide on a church with a pastor who has a huge following on Instagram? Does this church affirm everything about me? Such mentality runs the risk of pursuing a faith based on what God can do for us, forgetting what Christ has already accomplished.

---

6. McCracken, "Righteous Gemstones."

Social Gospel

There are other areas of false teaching to be wary of, including what has historically been known as the *social gospel*; related to, but not entirely synonymous with the term *social justice*. The nascent social gospel movement coincided with the progressive era of the late 1800s and early 1900s. This movement went beyond the idea of individual salvation and focused instead on the salvation, so to speak, of society. Seemingly more important than placing faith in Jesus Christ as the only redeemer for mankind were the scourges of poverty, drunkenness, abominable working conditions, and so forth. Instead of fighting these societal stains as part of pointing towards Jesus, the elimination of them became the goal itself. That is, better working conditions, fairer wages, and cleaner living saved society, and there was no higher objective.

Preachers and theologians like Friedrich Schleiermacher, Washington Gladden, Charles Monroe Sheldon, and Walter Rauschenbusch were also influential during this era. In *Recollections*, Gladden wrote, "I am fain to believe that the time is drawing near when the Christian Church will be able to discern and declare the simple truth that religion is nothing but Friendship, friendship with God and with all people."[7] Written towards the end of his life, Gladden, a Christian preacher, professed the chief end of religion to be friendship. This, of course, sells Jesus short.

As a part of the Neo-orthodoxy movement, Karl Barth, and later Reinhold Niebuhr, sharply criticized the social gospel. They took issue with a so-called Christianity that seemed to believe sin bubbled up from societal woes rather from the hearts of men.

Hand in hand with the social gospel, is, of course, social justice. For many readers, this term is just a regular part of one's vocabulary. The term was originally coined by Catholic scholar Luigi Taparelli d'Azeglio in 1840 and its concept was originally not much different than other branches of justice, such as criminal justice.

Now, I'm not about to go on a screed against social justice. Nor am I able to completely defend it. This is because it's a vague term that people can use to mean any number of things, many of which Christians should support, some of which they should not. Just because someone says they are doing "social justice" does not mean a Christian can be for the act or against the act without knowing what specific action is being undertaken.

---

7. Gladden, *Recollections*, 429.

Part 2: You Will Be Hated

I mention all this because any good works Christians engage in should be an outpouring of our service to Christ. Turning to James 2:14, we read, "What good is it, my brothers and sisters, if someone claims to have faith but does not have works? Can such faith save him?" A superficial reading of this passage might lead one to believe works are key to salvation, seemingly pitting James against Paul, who wrote to the Romans, "For we hold that one is justified by faith apart from works of the law" (Rom 3:28).

Does Paul contradict James? Of course not. Faith saves. What kind of faith? An active and alive faith. A faith that works through love (Gal 5:6). A faith that compels one to good works. A student in the Christian fellowship I advise was just expressing this. She said simply, "We do these things because we love Jesus."

Jesus himself said that you will know a Christian by his or her fruit (Matt 7:16). Now, we do not exchange a basket of fruit with God in order to purchase salvation. Salvation was already purchased by Jesus on the cross. We present this basket of fruit as an example of how our life changed by following Jesus. The fruit is evidence of our roots in Christ, not the roots themselves.

To place works ahead of faith is false teaching. Some churches may emphasize works more than faith, but that does not mean they are a bad church. Maybe they just need to take a step back and remind *why* they make it a point to pursue justice and mercy in their community. However, churches that completely disconnect their works from their faith should be avoided.

Legalism

Legalism takes correct orthodox teaching to the extreme and turns it into false teaching. Legalism claims the necessity of keeping the law to obtain or maintain one's salvation. This view would say you cannot be a Christian if you have engaged in sex outside of marriage, or, if you have done so as a Christian, you are no longer welcome in the church. The same for something like drunkenness.

We'll talk about the law more in a moment, but it's fair to recognize there are expectations of Christians to not do some things. Sinning without repentance or any desire to change is not good, and churches may even need to remove people from their congregation if this describes one of their attendees or members.

Legalism goes further. It says someone who engages in any sinful behavior (or, at least the sins they care about—when is the last time someone was excommunicated for gluttony?) is no longer a Christian. Or sometimes, anyone who has done one particularly evil and heinous (sarcasm alert!) sin, such as engage in same-sex relations or have an abortion, cannot possibly become a Christian. Churches who take this stance have a low view of the gospel.

Legalism also makes up new rules for Christians. The classic movie *Footloose* is a great example. Dancing was not permitted. Now, this seems pretty crazy to younger generations, although some of you may have grown up in churches or attended Christian schools that did not permit dancing. And, you know what? They kind of have a point. Think of your middle school or high school years when you got to have your body *really* close to your crush. There certainly was potential for hands to start roaming and to wind up in a pretty bad situation.

However, that made-up rule of "no dancing" is not found in the Bible. This is an example of a man-made rule creating new boundaries in order to follow a God-given command to not lust. But if following God-given commands does not save someone, than what does following man-made rules do? Again, the point isn't that we shouldn't set up boundaries for ourselves to help pursue holiness. The point is that if following these rules is what makes us Christians, than these rules have become legalism. And legalism is false teaching.

Other Heresies

You know, when I originally wrote this chapter, I just wanted to talk about the prosperity gospel. It's the easiest one to pick on! But there are many different types of false teachings young adults need to be aware of. Some are as old as Christianity itself. Here are just two more common ones.

One early heresy was Arianism. When it arose, it was very influential and led many people away from Christ. Arius argued that God the Father created Jesus, which is counter to Trinitarian teaching that the Father, Son, and Holy Spirit are all uncreated, eternal persons within the one being of God. It also places Jesus on a lower level than God the Father. It's a difficult concept to study, but Jesus is fully God and fully man (the fancy term for this is the hypostatic union) and Arianism denies this.

Why does this matter? A false view of Jesus distorts the power of the gospel. If Jesus is not on par with God, how can Jesus be worthy of being the sacrifice for sins? He wouldn't be. How would he be worthy of worship?

He wouldn't be. We may not drive down the road and see the First Arianism Church of De Moines, but this teaching exists in many churches. It's a prominent part of Jehovah's Witness theology.

Another heresy still alive today is Antinomianism. This teaches Christians are permitted to sin because we have been freed from the law. This false teaching believes that when Paul wrote we are no longer under the law (Rom 6:14) he meant we have no reason to abide by the law. However, this misses the first question Paul addresses in the chapter: Should Christians keep sinning since we're under grace? His response was an emphatic, "Absolutely not!" (Rom 6:2a, CSB).

Why does this matter? We'll discuss this more in chapter 13, but Christians who serve Christ pursue holiness. Yes, we are forgiven if we mess up and sin, but forgiveness implies there was wrongdoing. If we say we love Jesus, our natural inclination should be that we *want* to follow his commands. While the law no longer condemns us, it is still holy and we should still strive to follow it out of our love of Jesus.

Conclusion

J. Gresham Machen warned, "The greatest menace to the Christian Church to-day comes not from the enemies outside, but from the enemies within; it comes from the presence within the Church of a type of faith and practice that is anti-Christian to the core."[8] Machen is right because, as we discussed, persecution from outside of the church goes after our physical bodies. This persecution attempts to silence our Christian witness by excluding us from public life, bulldozing our buildings, or killing us. Yet, as unpleasant as all that is, we still have eternal life through Christ. It is the persecution from inside the church that tells us to conform to the world, to keep quiet about our faith, and to revise Jesus' words to make them more acceptable to the unbelieving world. Those actions might save our physical lives, but it is an attack on our very soul.

I know the last few chapters have been fairly gloomy and seemingly void of hope. That is not true, though. There is hope. For the Christian, there is always hope.

---

8. Machen, *Christianity and Liberalism*, 135.

11

But There Is Hope

Shortly before being arrested, Jesus was with his disciples. The mood was perhaps gloomy or despondent, as he spoke about sorrow and departing from them. Jesus taught, "Behold, the hour is coming, indeed it has come, when you will be scattered, each to his own home" (John 16:32). He was foretelling how each of them would abandon him in the coming hours. Yet, Jesus offered encouragement as well, continuing, "I have said these things to you, that in me you may have peace. *In the world you will have tribulation. But take heart; I have overcome the world*" (John 16:33, emphasis added).

It's as clear as clear can be: as Christ-followers, you and I will face tribulation. Times will be hard. Things will be difficult. We will lose friends. We will be looked at funny. Some of our businesses will be shut down. A few of us may even die just for professing the name of Jesus as savior in hostile regions around the world. Yet Jesus has overcome all of it. His life, death, and resurrection is the ultimate hope available.

After Jesus physically resurrected and was ascending to heaven, his final message was direct: "Go therefore and make disciples of all nations, baptizing them in the name of the Father and of the Son and of the Holy Spirit, teaching them to observe all that I have commanded you. And behold, I am with you always, to the end of the age" (Matt 28:19–20).

This is referred to as the Great Commission. Jesus commissioned us all to make disciples throughout the world. Keep in mind, Jesus has already told us (repeatedly) that by doing this we will be hated and possibly even killed. Reread that last sentence, though. Jesus is "with [us] always, to the end of the age." Despite those tribulations, wars and rumors

Part 2: You Will Be Hated

of wars, and all forms of persecution, Jesus is with us *always*. What greater hope could we have?

Consider what Paul Washer says: "Persecution has never hurt the church . . . only prosperity."[1] This makes sense when we don't look at the church as an organization to be advanced within society, gaining influence over government and media, but rather an unsinkable lifeboat on a stormy ocean void of any sign of land.

It is not the financial underpinnings of the American church saving souls and giving life; it is Jesus. That's not to say giving our money (as well as our time) isn't right. It is; doing such is a sacrifice of oneself to God. The problem is that we sometimes tend to think the bank accounts and worldly power of churches makes them great. We do not make the church great again by finding paths to the table of power, be it Washington, DC or elsewhere. The church is "great" when it serves God. Being prosperous can get in the way of that. Hiring folks to do something volunteers could do, building the steeple a little higher than anything else in town, electing the "right" person to office, or having a pastor who purchases himself a private jet or a 16,000-square-foot mansion can (and do) easily get in the way of promoting Christ to the world. Rather, these are examples of promoting the world and its pleasures to mankind.

Keeping in the mind that the church is not an earthly thing, but the united fellowship of Christ followers who are fellow heirs to eternal life, persecution should be less of a concern than prosperity. While prosperity can *distract us* from what's important, persecution *reminds us* of what's important. When we get shiny new things, we find comfort in them. When we are persecuted, we find comfort in Christ.

Further, we need to remember a thing or two about citizenship. Being a citizen of a country is more than just an address. Being a citizen of the United States means protection of a number of basic rights, such as speech, due process, and more. Most of us, especially those of us who are Christians, should recognize how much easier our lives are by just being citizens of a country like the United States versus being a citizen of Iran.

Yet as great as the United States is, those of us who are citizens of it need to admit that this citizenship is nothing compared to our citizenship in heaven. Paul encourages the Philippians to press onward towards righteousness in Christ and warns of those who are enemies of Christ and headed towards destruction. For the Christian, however, "our citizenship

---

1. Washer, *Christ, the True Vine*.

is in heaven, and from it we await a Savior, the Lord Jesus Christ, who will transform our lowly body to be like his glorious body, by the power that enables him even to subject all things to himself" (Phil 3:20–21).

Paul informs us we have been granted all rights and privileges that heaven can offer. As Christians, our souls are secure. Reformed theologians call this "the perseverance of the saints." This means our heavenly citizenship cannot be suspended or revoked, while our American (or Canadian, or British, or Honduran, etc.) citizenship will end once we die. We're stuck between what's often referred to as "the already" and "the not yet." This phrase explains that we are already a part of God's kingdom, but this kingdom has not yet been fully realized.

So while we need to understand there is work to be done here on Earth, persecution ought to trigger our kingdomly mindset. While youth will naturally lend itself to exciting and possibly even immature moments that are completely acceptable, we need to eschew the YOLO attitude. If "you only live once" then there is little meaning in that one life. However, we believe in eternal life, and as Russell Moore explains, "If Jesus is telling us the truth . . . our life planning ought to be about the next trillion years and beyond rather than just this moment." In addition, "We as Christians need to recover a holistic vision of what the kingdom of Jesus is and what it means for us both now and later. Unless we do, we will fundamentally misunderstand how this life relates to the next, and imagine that our earthly years are nothing more than a ferry to take us into eternity."[2]

So if our citizenship is in heaven, persecution is not our biggest concern. Persecution, at worst, only hastens our arrival home. Meanwhile, things like prosperity and false teaching serve to distract us and place hope in earthly trinkets or our own feelings, both of which are fleeting.

Remember, Jesus hates false teaching. He directly calls out the Nicolaitans in Revelation 2. The Nicolaitans wrongly held the belief that we were free to sin because we were freed from the law (remember antinomianism?). This is of course false, because Jesus came to fulfill the law and not to abolish it (Matt 5:17) and we are not to go on sinning so grace may abound (Rom 6:1). In Revelation, Jesus specifically addresses seven churches in Asia with both commendations and criticism, including the one in Ephesus. To this church's credit, they have staunchly opposed the Nicolaitans, and Jesus says to them, "you hate the works of the Nicolaitans, which I also hate" (Rev 2:6). Here Jesus affirms the importance of opposing false teaching.

---

2. Moore, "You Only Live Forever."

Part 2: You Will Be Hated

Persecution Grows the Kingdom

While we should not seek out persecution, it is worth reviewing what happens to the church when such pressure is placed on it.

We read in Acts that shortly after Jesus' ascension the apostles were gathered and the Holy Spirit descended upon them (what we call Pentecost). Led by Peter, the apostles continued preaching in the region and at one time added 3,000 to their number (Acts 2:41). This obviously did not make the Sadducees or Pharisees happy. Once while Peter and John were preaching, "the priests and the captain of the temple and the Sadducees came upon them, greatly annoyed because they were teaching the people and proclaiming in Jesus the resurrection from the dead. And they arrested them and put them in custody until the next day, for it was already evening" (Acts 4:1–3). The council ultimately could not find anything to charge them with, but threatened them to stop preaching, which Peter and John defiantly refused to do.

They, along with the rest of the apostles, were arrested again, but released later by an angel who instructed them to go preach in the temple. While the council continued to look for ways to stop them, more and more numbers were added to the ranks of believers. One believer, Stephen, was arrested and stoned to death, becoming the first Christian martyr. Consider what is happening here. We are looking at the beginning of a movement that has been met with resistance and death, yet that movement continued, and continues today. Despite persecution, the early church thrived.

A more recent example comes from Iran. If you recall from chapter 9, Iran is considered a restricted country for Christians. Voice of the Martyrs explains:

> Iran remains one of the most difficult nations in the world in which to be a Christian. Since President Hassan Rouhani took office in August 2013, the number of individuals in prison because of their beliefs has increased, and Christians are especially targeted. Over the past year, Iranian authorities have raided church services, threatened church members and arrested and imprisoned worshipers and church leaders, particularly Christian converts from Islam. Currently, there are approximately 90 Christians either in prison or awaiting trial.[3]

---

3. Voice of the Martyrs, *2017 Global Report*, 22.

Despite this, The Gospel Coalition reported in October 2016 that the efforts of Iran to shut down Christianity have backfired. Take, for an example, their attempt to destroy the Bible and warn its citizens against reading it. What is the typical human reaction when told not to read or watch something? You want to read or watch that something! The Iranian government is witnessing this response because, "Apparently, this warning has caused many Iranians, already disillusioned with their government, to become all the more eager to obtain a copy of the Bible. And many have put their faith in Christ after finding and reading a copy."[4]

The same goes for shutting down church buildings. Now, instead, Christians are meeting underground in homes, regularly adding to their numbers. Instead of several large church buildings, Iran is dealing with countless smaller congregations meeting everywhere. It is like trying to put out dozens and dozens of brushfires instead of one large, centralized fire. If you have brushfires all over the place, you have to send firefighters all over the place and it becomes difficult to coordinate efforts. And if you neglect one brushfire for the sake of another, soon that ignored brushfire is going to grow larger and larger.

The Christian Post reports that in Iran, "Hundreds are being baptized in large ceremonies and people are praising Jesus for saving them from despair and suicide." Around 20 years ago, "estimates put the number of believers in Iran at only 2,000–5,000 people, but new statistics are saying there could be anywhere between 300,000 to 1 million Christians in the country."[5] That's somewhere between a 600-percent and 5,000-percent increase under strict government persecution!

Conclusion

As Christians, we cannot fear persecution. For much of the world, this has been common practice. For Western and especially American Christians, this will be a new response. Let's let the blood of the martyrs influence our resolve in the face of persecution. While we do not seek out strife, let us always stand firm on the Word of God. Whatever happens from there happens. The church has always survived. Never forget that.

---

4. Yeghnazar, "5 Ways Persecution in Iran."
5. Zaimov, "Iran's House Church Movement."

Part 3

Love Them Anyway

12

Love Is a Verb

So young adult Christians are not to let others despise them. Yet we see the persecution of Christians abound throughout the world. In light of that, how are we to respond?

There are two questions I like to ask when I encounter and teach young Christians. First, what don't you do as a Christian that you would if you weren't a Christian? This is a little counterintuitive, but what things would you be doing if you were not following Christ? Consider your time, your money, your lifestyle, etc. Second, what *do* you do as a Christian that you wouldn't be doing if you weren't a Christian? Again, think of how your time and money are spent, the things you say, and the conflicts you have, and mentally highlight a few things. The underlying question is, *how is your life different because you are a Christian?*

James instructs us to be "doers of the word, and not hearers only" (Jas 1:22). That's because a genuine faith will manifest itself in what we do and say. If we are filled with the Holy Spirit, there should be character change taking place. The biggest character change is that we become more loving.

> By this we know that we abide in him and he in us, because he has given us of his Spirit. And we have seen and testify that the Father has sent his Son to be the Savior of the world. Whoever confesses that Jesus is the Son of God, God abides in him, and he in God. So we have come to know and to believe the love that God has for us. God is love, and whoever abides in love abides in God, and God abides in him. By this is love perfected with us, so that we may have confidence for the day of judgment, because as he is so also are we in this world. There is no fear in love, but perfect love casts out fear.

Part 3: Love Them Anyway

> For fear has to do with punishment, and whoever fears has not been perfected in love. We love because he first loved us. If anyone says, "I love God," and hates his brother, he is a liar; for he who does not love his brother whom he has seen cannot love God whom he has not seen. And this commandment we have from him: whoever loves God must also love his brother. (1 John 4:13–21)

John tells us if we claim to love God, but hate our brother, we are liars. We cannot love God if we hate those around us. For example, one of the sins of the American church is its historic complicity in slavery and its ongoing ignorance of racism. The hatred and exclusion of black Americans made many Christians liars. Again, the greatest character change an individual should experience when becoming a Christian is demonstration of love.

However, we need to be careful not to equate our actions with salvation. We cannot love our way into heaven. Faith alone saves us (Rom 3:28; 5:1; Gal 2:16; and Eph 2:8–9, among others). However, faith in Christ should generate a faith that is active in the world. James warns us, "faith by itself, if it does not have works, is dead" (Jas 2:17). Again, this doesn't mean there is any work you can do to earn your salvation. That's actually a false teaching. Rather, if you have genuine saving faith in Jesus Christ, your life will bear fruit as a testament to such.

Still, examine how James plays off of Paul. Paul writes in Romans 4 that Abraham was justified by his faith, yet James says in the second chapter of his letter that Abraham's faith was "completed" (ESV) or "made perfect" (KJV) through his works. Abraham's *works* didn't save him, his faith did; yet, *because he had faith*, he had works. Loving others will not save you, but if you have saving faith, you will love others. Paul writes that "faith working through love" is what we strive for (Gal 5:6). While our faith in Jesus Christ saves us, such a faith must result in love.

Paul also writes to the church in Galatia defining the fruit of the Spirit as, "*love*, joy, peace, patience, kindness, goodness, faithfulness, gentleness, [and] self-control" (Gal 5:22–23). He tells the church in Corinth, "If I speak in the tongues of men and angels, but have not love, I am a noisy gong or clanging cymbal. And if I have prophetic powers, and understand all mysteries and all knowledge, and if I have all faith, so as to remove mountains, but have not love, I am nothing. If I give away all I have, and if I deliver up my body to be burned, but have not love, I gain nothing" (1 Cor 13:1–3). Paul further describes love as "patient and kind," "not arrogant or rude," "rejoic[ing] in truth]," and "never end[ing]," concluding this section of his letter by saying, "faith, hope, and love abide, these three; but the greatest of these is love" (1 Cor 13:13).

You cannot be a Christian and not love. Here's the problem, though: What *is* love? There are books titled *Love Wins*. We read of hashtag activism such as #LoveIsLove. Many of our Christian friends will say that all we need to do is love. And while that's true, *what does that mean*? Sadly, many professing Christians will take this to mean that we become a passive, affirming congregation that bites its collective tongue when it comes to sin. The Bible tells us to love, yes, but it also instructs us on what that should look like. Christians who eschew doctrine tell us to love, but miss out that this same doctrine instructs us on what that means and what it should look like.

Whom Do You Love?

To know whom to love, start with Mark 12:28-31:

> And one of the scribes came up and heard them disputing with one another, and seeing that he answered them well, asked him, "Which commandment is the most important of all?" Jesus answered, "The most important is, 'Hear, O Israel: The Lord our God, the Lord is one. And you shall love the Lord your God with all your heart and with all your soul and with all your mind and with all your strength.' The second is this: 'You shall love your neighbor as yourself.' There is no other commandment greater than these."

So the greatest commandment is to love God and the second greatest commandment is to love others. Remember that order.

Sometimes folks erroneously claim Jesus taught that the most important thing is to love others, but we can see in Scripture this is incorrect. Above everything, we are to love God. Now, loving God does not negate loving others, but to frame the gospel message as one that only teaches us to love others is incorrect. Further, as I already asked, what does it mean to love anyway?

This is where the last several chapters will take us: What is love? We need to understand this if we are to engage the world with Christian love. Love is not a pop song. Love is not affirming sin that separates one from Jesus, regardless of whether that places us on "the wrong side of history" or not. Nor do we disregard our command to love when the would-be recipient of that love has different politics than us or unbiblical views on various issues.

Part 3: Love Them Anyway

Love does not always look like love. Would you say slapping my toddler's hand looks like love? Context should help decide. Over Christmas when my daughter was one year old, she was obsessed with our Christmas tree, especially the giant lightbulbs. It's important to know for this story that my precious little girl has never been gentle. She would grab the bulbs pretty roughly in her little hands and squeeze. The danger, of course, was shards of plastic cutting up those little hands. So I slapped those little hands instead. Disciplining her to not do something potentially very dangerous is love, even if it doesn't look like it.

Context matters. A so-called Christian message that says "just love" is not enough. We need more context to know what that means.

13

Love God

Remember: "The most important [commandment] is, 'Hear, O Israel: The Lord our God, the Lord is one. And you shall love the Lord your God with all your heart and with all your soul and with all your mind and with all your strength.'"

So the most important thing for a Christian to do is to love God. Not only that, but love him with all our heart, with all our soul, with all our mind, and with all our strength. That's not an easy task, and a lifetime is not long enough to perfect it. Still, it's what we are called to. But why? *Why* do we love God?

"We love because he first loved us." (1 John 4:19)

It's pretty much that simple. We love God because he first loved us. Our existence, the blessings we regularly receive, and, most importantly, salvation through Jesus Christ are all examples of his unrelenting love for us. He reached out to us, showed us his glory, and we respond the only way we ought: we love him.

Imagine living every day setting aside time to marvel at God's love for you. You do not have to exist, but you do. Some of you may be experiencing anxiety, depression, loss, illness, or more, and it's hard to see God as good. But it is that goodness that has breathed you into existence, and it is that goodness that has granted you a second birth in Christ. God has given both life *and* eternal life. Whatever happens in between is a bonus.

Psalm 16:1–2 cries out, "Preserve me, O god, for in you I take refuge. I say to the Lord, 'You are my Lord; I have no good apart from you.'" We love because he first loved us. But how should we respond to that love? How can we love God back? I can think of at least four good places to start:

1. Believe
2. Pray
3. Study Scripture
4. Follow his commands

Believe

We need to trace our belief in God back to Genesis 15. The word of the Lord visited Abram (later renamed by God as Abraham) in a vision. God spoke to him, saying, "Fear not, Abram, I am your shield; your reward shall be great." Abram lamented to God his lack of children, thus having no heir. God then led "him outside and said, 'Look toward heaven, and number the stars, if you are able to number them.' Then he said to him, 'So shall your offspring be.' *And he believed the Lord, and he counted it to him as righteous*" (Gen 15:1, 5–6, emphasis added).

God reached into Abram's life and made him a promise, and Abram believed. This moment is recognized as the Abrahamic Covenant. What is a covenant? Mark Jones describes it like this:

> Scholars have defined *covenant*—translated from the Hebrew *berith* and the Greek *diathēke*—in various ways, and the context in which the word is used in Scripture will also inform our understanding of its meaning. At its most basic level, a covenant is an oath-bound relationship between two or more parties . . . In divine covenants, God sovereignly establishes the relationship with His creatures. There are other nuances, but a divine covenant given after the fall is, fundamentally, one in which God binds Himself by His own oath to keep His promises.[1]

God made a covenant to Abram, and Abram believed God.

Fast-forward to a Pharisee named Nicodemus coming to see Jesus at night in order not to be noticed. Nicodemus is not showing up to criticize or silence Jesus, but to learn from him. He doesn't want to deal with the rest of the Pharisees' harassing questions of him should he be seen with Jesus, but he is willing to at least take a small risk by going at night. Jesus responds

---

1. Jones, "What Is a Covenant?"

to some of Nicodemus's questions, and eventually goes into the first Bible verse many of us ever memorized:

> For God so loved the world, that he gave his only Son, that whoever believes in him should not perish but have eternal life. For God did not send his Son into the world to condemn the world, but in order that the world might be saved through him. Whoever believes in him is not condemned, but whoever does not believe is condemned already, because he has not believed in the name of the only Son of God." (John 3:16–18)

The first thing we need to do to show God our love is to believe him. Believe who he is, believe his promises, believe in his son, and believe in his sovereignty. The most basic way to love God is to recognize his place on the throne above all creation. Certainly, there are details to work out after that, but this is the first step. Many of you reading this book have already done this. However, some of you are just coming around to this idea. I urge you to seek out a pastor, an elder, a Christian professor, or someone else you know who has been a dedicated Christ follower for a few years. Allow them to go more in depth with you and help you submit to God's glory.

Pray

In Question 98, the Westminster Shorter Catechism defines prayer as "an offering up of our desires unto God, for things agreeable to his will, in the name of Christ, with confession of our sins, and thankful acknowledgement of his mercies." In other words, prayer is a time to make our desires known (while recognizing those desires ought to conform to God's will), confess our sins, and thank God for his gifts and mercies, most notably salvation through Jesus Christ.

Scripture is saturated in prayer, man's direct connection to God. Moses prayed. David prayed. Mary prayed. Jesus prayed. Paul prayed. Peter prayed. Are you praying?

Scroll through the Psalms and you will see a number of examples of David crying out to God in joy, in angst, in worship, in fear, and in confusion. Just before he was arrested, Jesus prayed in the garden of Gethsemane with so much agony that he sweat blood (Luke 22:44). Scripture records many of our great men of women of faith as individuals who prayed.

In Matthew 6, Jesus teaches how to pray, and even gives us a model, known as the Lord's Prayer:

Part 3: Love Them Anyway

> Our Father in heaven,
> Hallowed by your name.
> Your kingdom come,
> Your will be done,
> On earth as it is in heaven.
> Give us this day our daily bread,
> And forgive us our debts,
> As we also have forgiven our debtors.
> And lead us not into temptation,
> But deliver us from evil. (Matt 6:9–13)

Jesus exhibits five key components to prayer: worship (v. 9b), recognition of God's lordship (v. 10), requests for our needs (v. 11), asking and granting forgiveness (v. 12), and requests for strength to persevere (v.13).

Prayer saturates Scripture. Communicating to God through prayer is an essential way to demonstrate love for God. Sometimes prayer will bring you to your knees in tears begging for God to forgive you or to guide discernment on a difficult matter. Other times it's a moment of serenity with a good cup of coffee and a beautiful sunrise that causes you to close your eyes and whisper, "Thank you, Lord." God is never further than a prayer away.

Study Scripture

The difference between *studying* Scripture and *reading* Scripture is monumental. When we read, we recognize the words gaining at best a surface-level cognizant awareness. When we study we also pour effort into *comprehending* what we read. We make connections to current knowledge and other readings, we look up context and history, we analyze maps and archaeological findings, and we spend time thinking through the text's impact.

For example, if you *read* the story of the woman at the well (John 4), you learn that that Jesus impressed a woman by speaking of things about her that he shouldn't have known. When you *study* this passage, you recognize that the woman purposely went to the well at a time when no one else should be there, learn about the cultural impact of a Jew interacting with a Samaritan woman, and connect the concept of "living water" with additional Scripture in Isaiah 12, Zechariah 14, John 7, and elsewhere.

Reading Scripture is passive. Studying Scripture is active. And the study of Scripture is imperative. Kevin DeYoung writes, "As the people of God, we believe the word of God can be trusted in every way to speak

Love God

what is true, command what is right, and provide us with what is good."[2] We should view the Bible as the greatest source of truth and as inspired by God. While we ought to avoid legalism in saying that a Christian must read *x* amount of Scripture every day, a genuine faith should compel us to want to dig deep into the Bible, spending more and more time in the word.

Consider Matthew 4. Jesus is fasting in the wilderness when Satan comes to him. Scripture records three times Satan tempts Jesus, and each time Jesus responds with Scripture. If the Son of God was so dedicated to Scripture that he used it to rebut Satan, we should heed this example. We previously discussed the danger of false teaching. The best way to combat it is to know Scripture better. If you want to love and serve God, studying Scripture is essential.

Studying Scripture isn't easy, and there will be plenty of times you will be confused. I recommend a few things. First, use resources like solid commentaries (I'm enjoying the *Christ-Centered Exposition* series) and a Bible atlas. These resources do not *replace* Scripture, but may help you understand it better. Second, get connected with someone who knows more Scripture than you do, but doesn't flaunt it. Specifically, look to the ranks of pastors, elders, and professors. Share your questions and insights with them. Third, do not dismiss Scripture that confuses you or does not make sense. Instead, struggle with it. Remember Paul's words to Timothy: "All Scripture is God-breathed and is useful for teaching, rebuking, correcting and training in righteousness, so that the servant of God may be thoroughly equipped for every good work" (2 Tim 3:16–17, NIV). It might not make sense to you at the time, but that does not mean it's useless.

The ability to study Scripture is paramount. One of the best free resources I know is the Blue Letter Bible app. It's not as slick or fancy as other Bible apps out there, but it connects you to solid commentaries and what is called an interlinear. An interlinear allows you to view the English translation from the original language, be it Hebrew, Greek, or Aramaic. This allows you to see how the original word was translated in different sections of Scripture and review the range of meanings the word has. How we interpret Scripture has a direct impact on what we believe and how we live out our faith. I am convinced our ability to interpret Scripture is more important than our ability to memorize Scripture.

---

2. DeYoung, *Taking God at His Word*, 18.

Part 3: Love Them Anyway

Follow God's Commands

A fourth way to love God is to follow his commands. To expand on this, I need to make two seemingly conflicting points: We should all follow God's commands, but no one can keep all of God's commands. Supporting Scripture:

> Whoever has my commands and keeps them is the one who loves me. The one who loves me will be loved by my Father, and I to will love them and show myself to them. (John 14:21, NIV)

And:

> For all have sinned and fall short of the glory of God. (Rom 3:23)

The Bible shouldn't be viewed as a rulebook, but, yes, there are a lot of rules in it. We are instructed to remain chaste, to care for widows and orphans, to avoid drunkenness, and plenty more. God commands his people to do some things, and to not do other things. We cannot ignore that.

However, we also recognize, as a fallen people, we are incapable of being completely sin-free. This is the whole point of Jesus' life, death, and resurrection. If we were capable of being sinless, the blood on the cross would not have been necessary. Yet the cedar poles were stained crimson. This tells us we cannot save ourselves, and because of our sins we deserve death. The law informs us we are sinners, and grace sets us free.

With that said, get ready for a whole lot of Romans. Paul instructs us to "uphold the law" (Rom 3:31), calling it "holy" (Rom 7:12), while knowing full well that "none is righteous, no, not one" (Rom 3:10). However, the good news is, "Sin will have no dominion over [us], since [we] are not under the law but under grace" (Rom 6:14). This may raise the question: If I am under grace, does sin no longer matter? Or, is sin, as one church I've seen argues, not that big a deal? Paul answers, "So you also must consider yourselves dead to sin and alive to God in Christ Jesus" (Rom 6:11), and reminds us, "the wages of sin is death, but the free gift of God is eternal life in Christ Jesus our Lord" (Rom 6:23). Sin is a very big deal, but Jesus has conquered it.

And since it is a big deal, a life in Christ means we distance ourselves from it. Kevin DeYoung boldly proclaims, "No matter what you profess, if you show a disregard for Christ by giving yourself over to sin—impenitently and habitually—then heaven is not your home."[3] Clearly he isn't

---

3. DeYoung, *Hole in Our Holiness*, 14.

Love God

saying that if you sin you don't go to heaven. That contradicts the work of Jesus on the cross. However, living a Christian life means we repent of our sin and we go back to it less and less as we grow in holiness.

We have to acknowledge both these truths at the same time: being a Christian means we stop doing some things in our lives (watching porn, lying, etc.) and start doing others (tithing, putting the needs of others before our own, etc.), but grace alone saves us.

All of this matters because if we want to change hearts and minds about Jesus, be it in the West or regions more hostile to the gospel, it begins with our own personal renewal. If we want others to believe Jesus can change their lives, we need to live as though he is changing our own. Following the Bible's commands, be it caring for the poor and loving refugees or pursuing holiness in areas related to sex, is part of our public witness.

It's okay to admit following God's commands isn't always easy. I imagine that's partially the point. For example, being a Christian would be a lot easier in the Western world if homosexuality wasn't a sin. You and I can try to rationalize why God made this decree, but ultimately what matters is that *it is a decree from God*. We may not want to follow His commands, but let's remember that God is good (Ps 136:1; Mark 10:18, and elsewhere) and his commandments are "holy, righteous, and good" (Rom 7:12). Loving God means, in part, keeping his commands.

Also, keep in mind what we have gained through Jesus. Sacrificing areas of our lives is nothing compared to what God has given us. A.W. Tozer wrote:

> The man who has God for his treasure has all things in One. Many ordinary treasures may be denied him, or if he is allowed to have them, the enjoyment of them will be so tempered that they will never be necessary to his happiness. Or if he must see them go, one after one, he will scarcely feel a sense of loss, for having the Source of all things he has in One all satisfaction, all pleasure, all delight. Whatever he may lose he has actually lost nothing, for he now has it all in One, and he has it purely, legitimately and forever.[4]

No, following God's commands is not always easy, but whatever temporary loss we think we suffer from it, we have gained much more for eternity. His commands are often difficult, and sometimes one of the most difficult is to love others.

---

4. Tozer, *Pursuit of God*, 25–26.

14

Love Others

"The second is this: 'You shall love your neighbor as yourself.'" (Mark 12:31)

Jesus states that the second greatest commandment is to love your neighbor as yourself. This may seem pretty simple and straightforward, but it might trigger this question: Who is my neighbor? Jesus was actually asked this very question, and he responded with one of the most well-known parables:

> But he, desiring to justify himself, said to Jesus, "And who is my neighbor?" Jesus replied, "A man was going down from Jerusalem to Jericho, and he fell among robbers, who stripped him and beat him and departed, leaving him half dead. Now by chance a priest was going down that road, and when he saw him he passed by on the other side. So likewise a Levite, when he came to the place and saw him, passed by on the other side. But a Samaritan, as he journeyed, came to where he was, and when he saw him, he had compassion. He went to him and bound up his wounds, pouring oil and wine. Then he set him on his own animal and brought him to an inn and took care of him. And the next day he took out two denarii and gave them to the innkeeper, saying, 'Take care of him, and whatever more you spend, I will repay you when I come back.' Which of these three, do you think, proved to be a neighbor to the man who fell among the robbers?" He said, "The one who showed him mercy." And Jesus said to him, "You go, and do likewise." (Luke 10:29–37)

Love Others

The Samaritan saw someone who needed help, and helped him. He was loving towards the person dying along the road he was traveling. The dying man entered the Samaritan's life, making himself a neighbor.

If your neighbor is any person you come in contact with, this includes your boss. It includes your professor. It includes your roommate, and the person living next door. It includes that jerk frat guy in your class. It includes the flaming liberal in your class. It includes the racist nationalist in your class. It includes that ex-boyfriend who cheated on you. It includes everyone you come in contact with, be it in person or online. It's an exhaustive list, and it can be exhausting thinking about loving all the people you don't want to love. But, keep in mind, our neighbors also include our enemies.

Jesus taught, "You have heard that it was said, 'You shall love your neighbor and hate your enemy.' But I say to you, love your enemies and pray for those who persecute you, so that you may be sons of your Father who is in heaven." (Matt 4:43–44). This is revolutionary. Common sense would indicate that if someone out there hates you, there really is no reason to love them. They hate you? Hate them back, right? Jesus says otherwise, explaining, "For if you love those who love you, what reward do you have? Do not even the tax collectors do the same? And if you greet only your brothers, what more are you doing than others? Do not even the Gentiles do the same?" (Matt 5:46–47).

Jesus gets right to his point: What's the big deal about loving people you like? That's pretty basic. The issue is, as Christians, we are supposed to do better. We are supposed to love our enemies and pray for those who persecute us, so very clearly our enemies are our neighbors as well. It's a radical love.

Loving others is first and foremost lowering and humbling ourselves. We can't love others well unless we start from a perspective of placing another's life ahead of our own. In Mark 9:35, Jesus catches his disciples arguing over who is the greatest among them. Jesus corrects them, saying, "If anyone would be first, he must be last of all and servant of all." To love others as we are called to do, we must see everyone else as individuals to serve.

Okay, we are to love everyone. But *how* can we love others? Although there are countless ways to love someone, here are five simple and biblical ways to get started:

1. Forgive
2. Give

Part 3: Love Them Anyway

3. Be kind
4. Be truthful
5. Share the gospel

Forgive

Forgiveness is an essential Christian concept. When Peter asks how often he should forgive someone who sins against him, Jesus offers up the parable of the unforgiving servant to illustrate:

> "Therefore the kingdom of heaven may be compared to a king who wished to settle accounts with his servants. When he began to settle, one was brought to him who owed him ten thousand talents. And since he could not pay, his master ordered him to be sold, with his wife and children and all that he had, and payment to be made. So the servant fell on his knees, imploring him, 'Have patience with me, and I will pay you everything.' And out of pity for him, the master of that servant released him and forgave him the debts. But when that same servant went out, he found one of his fellow servants who owed him a hundred denarii, and seizing him, he began to choke him, saying, 'Pay what you owe.' So his fellow servant fell down and pleaded with him, 'Have patience with me, and I will pay you.' He refused and went and put him in prison until he should pay the debt. When his fellow servants saw what had taken place, they were greatly distressed, and they went and reported to their master all that had taken place. Then his master summoned him and said to him, 'You wicked servant! I forgave you all that debt because you pleaded with me. And should not you have had mercy on your fellow servant, as I had mercy on you?' And in anger his master delivered him to the jailers, until he should pay all his debt. So also my heavenly Father will do to every one of you, if you do not forgive your brother from your heart."
> (Matt 18:23–35)

This servant owed his master a hefty sum, yet the master took compassion on him. Right after, the servant finds a fellow servant who owes him a considerably less figure. Instead of passing along the forgiveness, he choked him and had him thrown in prison for not paying. Not to belabor the point, but in this parable the master is God and we are the unforgiving servant. The other servant is anyone we are refusing to forgive. Every sin you have committed, be it through commission or omission, is an offense to God. Instead of holding believers accountable to all those sins, the work of Jesus Christ cancelled them for his followers. God has forgiven Christians their sins and will forgive future sins. Therefore, if you are a Christian, the bitterness you hold against another is hypocritical and sinful.

The end of this parable should place a healthy fear in us. The master delivered the unforgiving servant over to the jailers because he failed to appreciate the forgiveness he himself received, as demonstrated by not passing along the forgiveness. Jesus then explained that his "heavenly Father will do to every one of you, if you do not forgive your brother from your heart." That is, you will be tossed aside and sent away from the Master. Not forgiving others sets us on the path to hell.

Paul adds his thoughts on forgiveness, writing, "Put on then, as God's chosen ones, holy and beloved, compassionate hearts, kindness, humility, meekness, and patience, bearing with one another and, if one has a complaint against another, forgiving each other; as the Lord has forgiven you, so you must also forgive" (Col 3:12–13).

If we want to love others, we need to forgive them. However, any discussion of forgiveness must include what forgiveness isn't: Forgiveness alone is not the same as reconciliation. In Christ, we should always hope that forgiveness can lead to reconciliation, but it doesn't always. Forgiving someone for wrecking your car doesn't mean you hand her the keys as soon as it's out of the shop. Forgiving an abusive father does not mean moving back in with him. Forgiving a sexual abuser does not mean dropping legal charges.

While all relationships can be made new through Christ, many times it just won't happen. Shane Pruitt points out, "We're commanded by Scripture to forgive others, love others, and be kind to others; however, nowhere in Scripture are we commanded to be friends with everyone."[1] I think this is a fair point, but enough of what forgiveness isn't. Instead, what *does* forgiveness look like?

John Piper identifies seven key components to forgiveness:

1. Resisting revenge
2. No returning evil for evil
3. Wishing them well
4. Grieving at their calamities

---

1. Pruitt, *9 Common Lies*, 88.

Part 3: Love Them Anyway

5. Praying for their welfare
6. Seeking reconciliation so far as it depends on you
7. Coming to their aid in distress[2]

The first two focus on not causing harm to the other person and the next three emphasize having positive thoughts for them. These are not easy, but I believe in most instances we understand this call and with prayer and guidance we can reach them. The last two, however, are the most difficult.

As previously stated, forgiveness isn't the same as reconciliation. Reconciliation requires both parties to seek out peace, and that isn't always the case. Sometimes you will forgive someone without them ever even knowing they wronged you. Further, reconciliation doesn't mean that trust has been restored; that can take years, if it ever happens. If a friend swiped your wallet while he was in your room, it's not unreasonable to not allow him in your room alone anymore, even if you've forgiven him.

Coming to the aid of someone who has wronged you when they are in distress may be even more difficult. It's one thing to not harm them or to not think negatively of them; it's quite another to actively help them. Now, there are extremes here. For example, if you see an ex-boyfriend in the dining hall choking on chicken wing, you should do the Heimlich maneuver or at least call for help if you don't know how. That should be obvious. On the flip side, if someone has stolen money from you to buy tickets to a concert, and you later find out he needs to drop out of school because he can't afford tuition, I would argue you are under no obligation to arrange a GoFundMe page. Of course, doing so would be an incredible example of loving someone.

Give

To give is to sacrifice. When you give something, you're taking something that is rightfully yours and handing it over to another's possession. This is different than offering favors. When you do someone a favor, there's an expectation, often unstated, that the other individual will do something for you later on. There is nothing wrong with trading your time, talents, or money for a later, unidentified return. But that is not a gift to another, and it is not what Scripture calls us to do.

2. Piper, *As We Forgive Our Debtors*.

Let's consider two things everyone should give: money and time. You may have more of one than the other, and I recognize that some folks just do not have much money. I readily acknowledge that many readers of this book are college students with little cash on hand. That's fine, but if that's you, you are still capable of giving time and a portion of whatever money you *do* have.

When it comes to giving money, Proverbs 3:9 instructs us to "Honor the Lord with [our] wealth and with the first fruits of all [our] produce." I cannot instruct on how much to give. There is no raw number to tell you, because God doesn't need your money; he desires your sacrifice as an expression of love. This probably raises at least two questions. First, are we good as long as we tithe 10 percent? For example, if you make $40,000 a year and give $4,000 a year, that's good, right? Maybe. Or, maybe it's just a good start.

Second, where should your money go? If you plan on tithing at 10 percent, can you give 5 percent to your local church and the other 5 percent to a charity like World Vision, Samaritan's Purse, International Justice Mission, or a local camping ministry? John Piper addresses both of these questions. "No, the tithe, ten percent of your income, is not a 'have to' in the New Testament," Piper explains. He cites Romans 7:6 as freeing us from the law, and 2 Corinthians 8:3 and 9:6–7 as instructing us to give according to our means and what has been decided in our heart. Piper continues:

> So the point is not that we be governed by percentages. They are not mandated. Rather, we should be governed by lavish sacrificial generosity that overflows freely and joyfully. So I have often said to my people over the years that a middle-class American who is only tithing ten percent is probably robbing God. In other words, we have become so accustomed to our Western prosperity and its ways of life that we think five or ten percent is generous.[3]

As far as *where* our money should go, Piper again clarifies that there is no set rule on the matter. "The largeness of your heart, the biblical centrality of the local church, and the wonderful value of other ministries decide the question." However, keep in mind, "the one institution in the world that is clearly rooted in the New Testament and in the gospel is the local church. If that institution fails, all other ministries become ineffective." Ultimately, you are expected to sacrifice your money to further God's kingdom and to take care of others. It's a good idea to give *at least* 10 percent, but it's not

---

3. Piper, "May I Split My Giving" (podcast episode)

required. It's important that a good chunk of what you give is given to the local church, but, again, it's not required.

Further, I would argue that we should all be prepared to give to those in need who are around us. Someone nearby loses their home in a fire? Give. A family's medical expenses involving a sick child are accumulating? Give. These are the needs that arise when we least expect it. My wife and I are friends with a couple who have a separate checking account for just such occasions. When a need comes up they don't stress over how they can give, for they have already prepared for it. That's living a sacrificial life in order to love others.

Additionally, we can draw even more wisdom from C. S. Lewis, who wrote in *Mere Christianity*:

> I do not believe one can settle how much we ought to give. I am afraid the only safe rule is to give more than we can spare. In other words, if our expenditure on comforts, luxuries, amusements, etc., is up to the standard common among those with the same income as our own, we are probably giving away too little. If our charities do not at all pinch or hamper us, I should say they are too small. There ought to be things we should like to do and cannot do because our charities expenditure excludes them.[4]

That is to say, there should probably be things you want to do or own that you do not do or own because you have so prioritized tithing and offering money. For some, this may mean having a nice vacation at Virginia Beach instead of a Caribbean island. Others might be driving a 2008 RAV4 instead of a 2018 Toyota Tundra. And some of you may be making coffee at home four or five days a week to take into work instead of stopping at Dunkin every day.

One final point on giving money: being poor (including being a poor college student) is not an excuse to not give *something*. Mark 12:41–44 records:

> And [Jesus] sat down opposite the treasury and watched the people putting money into the offering box. Many rich people put in large sums. And a poor widow came and put in two small copper coins, which make a penny. And he called his disciples to him and said to them, "Truly, I say to you, this poor widow has put in more than all those who are contributing to the offering box. For they all

---

4. Lewis, *Mere Christianity*, 86.

contributed out of their abundance, but she out of her poverty has put in everything she had, all she had to live on."

You might not have *much* to give, but you are still called to give.

However, if you are only capable of dropping a couple bucks in the plate on Sundays, you may have *time* to give. Psalm 74:16 says to God, "Yours is the day, Yours also is the night." Like our finances, our time is a gift from God. Whatever is in our bank account, and however many days we have left, only belong to us by way of the Father. Our local church and local community need us.

Serving in the local church may be something lofty like praying before the congregation. Other times it may mean walking the aisle and making sure the offering plate gets to the next row. Or, perhaps, it might be staying late to empty all the trash cans. All these jobs need to be done, and you are not above any of them.

I can also guarantee there is work to be done in your local community, organized or unorganized. Food cupboards and soup kitchens need workers. Your elderly widowed neighbor needs her lawn cut. The glass bottle the waste management folks dropped on your road needs cleaned up. All of this takes time, and all of this is some form of service. Placing the need of the hungry, the elderly, and your neighbors before yourself is a sacrifice of time, and it's what you are called to do.

It's too easy to be lazy and just let someone else to do the work. Scripture has strong words for the lazy:

> The sluggard buries his hand in the dish and will not even bring it back to his mouth. (Prov 10:24)

> The sluggard says, "There is a lion on the road! There is a lion in the streets!" (Prov 26:13. Note: there isn't *really* a lion, the sluggard is just making ridiculous excuses.)

> If anyone is not willing to work, let him not eat. (2 Thess 3:10)

Don't be so lazy you can't get your hand out of the bowl of popcorn. Don't be so lazy you make up excuses about a lion running through your suburban development. Don't refuse to help when you can and then expect to reap rewards. I know your time is valuable. Trust me, I jealously guard my time, and it's sinful. My time is not my own; it's God's. And I need to offer it back to him through service, and so should you.

Part 3: Love Them Anyway

Be Kind

Being kind means using words and showing actions that demonstrate a gentle, considerate, generous, and compassionate nature. There will be times when we have to stand against something, but we should do so from a position of humility.

Paul writes to the church in Colossae, "Let your speech always be gracious, seasoned with salt, so that you may know how you ought to answer each person" (Col 4:6). When we speak to folks both inside and outside the church about a difficult matter, there is a good way to do it and a bad way. The good way is to be kind, recognizing your own sinfulness. The issue is not the person you are speaking to, but that we live in a fallen world where all fall short of the glory of God. The other person may be woefully wrong on the matter, but you have previously been woefully wrong yourself. Did you change your mind when someone screamed at you, belittled you in front of others, and made you feel like garbage? Probably not. Standing firm on the Word of God and compassionately and *kindly* speaking with someone you disagree with will go much further.

This includes speaking to individuals outside of the church. Consider social media debates. Often, folks on social media are just looking for a fight. They have no intention of convincing you to turn away from your faith; they just want to make you look foolish in front of others. Flip this around and, instead of making someone else look foolish by being a jerk, be overly kind and humble in your responses (Prov 25:21–22). If the other person continues to get angrier and more sarcastic, they will make themselves look foolish. Onlookers may not agree with you, but they will recognize your heart, which may open up their hearts later on.

It's difficult to love someone without being kind. Paul lists kindness as one of the fruits of the spirit (Gal 5:22) and writes to the church in Ephesus, "Let all bitterness and wrath and anger and clamor and slander be put away from you, along with all malice. Be kind to one another, tenderhearted, forgiving one another, as God in Christ forgave you" (Eph 4:31–32). It's not always easy, but demonstrating kindness should be part of your public witness, and it is an obvious way to love another person.

Love Others

Be Truthful

I see two key points to being truthful. First, don't lie, and second, speak truth. The first is passive, because the point is you *don't* do something. The second is active, because you *do* do something.

As Christians, we all should recognize lying as sinful. Sin came into the world through deception when the serpent spoke trickery to Eve. The ninth commandment says, "You shall not bear false witness against your neighbor" (Exod 20:16). God instructs in Leviticus 19:11–12, "You shall not steal; you shall not deal falsely; you shall not lie to one another. You shall not swear by my name falsely, and so profane the name of your God: I am the Lord." Proverbs 12:22 tells us, "The Lord detests lying lips, but he delights in people who are trustworthy." In John 8, Jesus tells the Pharisees they are children of Satan because they lie, and Satan "was a murderer from the beginning, and does not stand in the truth, because there is no truth in him. When he lies, he speaks out of his own character, for he is a liar and the father of lies" (John 8:44).

When stacking up Scripture about lying, observe how seriously the issue it taken. Sin entered the world through deceit. Not lying is one of the Ten Commandments. God "detests" falsehood. Satan is "the father of lies." This is all very serious stuff, and if we're being truthful, we are often not very truthful.

I can't count the times I have lied to hide my failures or avoid embarrassment. I've lied over dumb stuff. For instance, I love books and Amazon is way too easy for me to access. I will order a book on Tuesday just because and then try to hide it from my wife. Why do I do this? I'm ashamed that I'm spending too freely, even though my wife trusts me to be reasonable in my purchases. And to an extent, I'm not *that bad* about it, yet I still I do everything I can to hide it. I'll order something for our kids just so I can add a book into the package and slip it out when it arrives. I'll get my wife something a month before Valentine's Day just so I can include a new release for myself. All of this is deceitful, and God detests it. Who are you lying to? What are you lying about? You know the truth, and more importantly, God does.

Avoiding lies isn't the entirety of being truthful, though. Being truthful is actively speaking what is right and good into the world and into the lives that surround you. And what is truth? "Jesus said to [Thomas], 'I am the way, and the truth, and the life. No one comes to the Father except through me'" (John 14:6). You know how when you were a kid in Sunday school and the teacher asked a question and there was that other kid who always answered "Jesus" no matter the question? Well, scripturally, the answer to the question "What is truth" is, theologically speaking, "Jesus."

If we are speaking truth into a world that desperately needs it, our words should be Jesus' words. Words of love, forgiveness, gift, and kindness. Words that point back to the source of truth and the only path that leads to restoration. If we want to be truthful with those we love, those we work with, those we room with, and anyone else we come in contact with, then we need to direct them to Jesus.

Share the Gospel

If Jesus is the truth (which he is), then the greatest way we can love someone is to share the gospel with him or her. In fact, one famous atheist poses this paraphrased question: If you believe in the gospel of Jesus Christ, how much would you have to hate someone not to share it?

That famous atheist is Penn Jillette. And no, this story isn't a dramatic conversion story, as he remaind an avowed atheist. However, you can find a video on YouTube of him telling a story about a man who came up to him after a show. The gentleman praised Jillette's act and pulled out a Gideon's Bible, saying, "I brought this for you." The man explained that he was a businessman, was "sane," and understood that Jillette was an atheist. Jillette stresses how he appreciated the guy looking him in the eye while talking, as well as the fan's sincerity and kindness.

Jillette then explains to the viewer that he has "never respected" a religious believer who does not proselytize. Why? Why would a dedicated atheist not respect someone who doesn't share his faith? Penn Jillette does not believe in God, nor does he have much of anything kind to say about religion in general. Why *wouldn't* he want a Christian to keep his faith to himself? Jillette explains:

> If you believe that there's a heaven and a hell and people could be going to hell, or not getting eternal life, or whatever, and you think that "well, it's not really worth telling them this because it would make it socially awkward"... *How much do you have to hate somebody to not proselytize? How much do you have to hate somebody to believe that everlasting life is possible and not tell them?*[5]

---

5. Beinzee, "Gift of a Bible" (YouTube video), at 5:11. Emphasis added.

Love Others

Penn Jillette is not a Christian, but he gets that we profess belief in something of deep importance. If you and I truly believe the gospel message, how much would we have to hate someone not to share it? There is no better way to love someone than to share the gospel with them. There is no matter in existence more significant than eternity and where one spends it. We have the truth found in Jesus Christ. If you want to love someone, you need to share that truth with them.

Additionally, this is Jesus' last instruction to his disciples. As mentioned in chapter 11, Jesus left believers with the Great Commission, instructing his followers to "Go . . . and make disciples of all nations, baptizing them in the name of the Father and of the Son and of the Holy Spirit, teaching them to observe all that I have commanded you" (Matt 28:19–20). Acts 1:8 records Jesus informing his disciples they are tasked with being his "witnesses in Jerusalem and in all Judea and Samaria, and to the end of the earth." If these are the final instructions to Christ followers, it ought to resonate in our souls and convict our dealings with others. We are to love others and we can demonstrate it by sharing the gospel.

15

Sharing the Gospel

It's important to have common definitions of terms and ideas. So, what is the gospel?

To start, R. C. Sproul explains that the word used in Scripture for "gospel" is *euangelion*, having the "prefix eu-, which comes into English in a variety of words. We talk about euphonics or euphonious music, which refers to something that sounds good. We talk about a eulogy, which is a good word pronounced about someone at his or her funeral service. The prefix eu—refers to something good or pleasant. The word *angelos* or *angelion* is the word for 'message.'"[1] This is why *angels* are considered God's messengers. So "gospel" means "good message" or, more commonly, "good news." When we are sharing the gospel with someone, we are literally sharing good news.

Sproul also explains that we call our message "good news" because it is news about "the most serious problem that you and I have as human beings." That problem is this: "God is holy and He is just, and I'm not. And at the end of my life, I'm going to stand before a just and holy God, and I'll be judged. And I'll be judged either on the basis of my own righteousness—or lack of it—or the righteousness of another." And then here is where the good news comes in: "Jesus lived a life of perfect righteousness, of perfect obedience to God, not for His own well-being, but for His people. He has done for me what I couldn't possibly do for myself. But not only has He

---

1. Sproul, "What Does the Word 'Gospel' Mean?"

lived that life of perfect obedience, He offered Himself as a perfect sacrifice to satisfy the justice and righteousness of God."[2]

Greg Gilberts adds that pronouncing this good news essentially comes down to these four questions:

1. Who made us, and to whom are we accountable?
2. What is our problem?
3. What is God's solution to our problem?
4. How can I be included in the solution?[3]

Gilbert then explains that the Christian answers these four questions this way:

1. We are accountable to God.
2. Our problem is our sin against him.
3. God's solution is salvation through Jesus Christ.
4. We come to be included in that salvation by faith and repentance.

First Corinthians 15:3–4 reads: "For I delivered to you as of first importance what I also received: that Christ died for our sins in accordance with the Scriptures, that he was buried, that he was raised on the third day in accordance with the Scriptures."

Paul describes this gospel as of "first importance." That is, there is no more important message the Christian proclaims than Jesus dying for our sins and being buried only to rise on the third day. You have nothing to tell someone that is more important than the gospel message. Nothing. Absolutely nothing. Your opinions on predestination and free will are rubbish compared to the gospel. Baptizing by immersion or sprinkling is entirely irrelevant when placed against the gospel. If you place any secondary or tertiary issue ahead of the gospel message, you are spreading a false gospel.

Synthesize

If you are in the education field or majoring in the subject, the word "synthesize" should sound familiar. In 1956 Dr. Benjamin Bloom created his now-famous (at least in education circles) Bloom's Taxonomy. This outlined

2. Sproul, "What Is the Gospel?"
3. Gilbert, "What Is the Gospel?"

Part 3: Love Them Anyway

different types of learning, with the hope of encouraging higher levels of learning. For example, a lower level is simply "knowledge." That is, just remembering a fact learned, like that the Declaration of Independence was signed in 1776. One of the higher levels is "synthesis." This means creating something from what is learned, perhaps writing one's own version of a Declaration of Independence to secede and from your own country. For what we are talking about, it means finding your own words to accurately explain the gospel. Personally, I summarize the gospel as this:

1. God created us in his image and for his own desires.
2. Our sinful nature has separated us from God.
3. God's son, Jesus Christ, being both fully God as well as fully man, lived the perfect life and became the final sacrifice for sins.
4. Those (and only those) who repent, confessing faith in Jesus as their savior are 1) reconciled with God, and 2) filled with the Holy Spirit for guidance.

That's not some magical or perfect way of explaining the gospel, but it hits the key points, answering all of Gilbert's questions. It is also in my own language, in words and vernacular I use every day (as opposed to the word "vernacular," which I use here to impress you).

I would recommend you to find a way to explain the gospel simply and in your own language, given that it follows a similar basic format and remains doctrinally sound. There is nothing wrong per se about memorizing another's words, given that it is still biblical. If you know exactly how Tim Keller or Russell Moore summarizes the gospel message, you could do a lot worse. However, possessing the ability to paraphrase or synthesize the critical elements of the gospel into your regular language demonstrates a deeper understanding of it. This also better prepares you to answer questions, whereas trying to use another's words may make it more difficult to do so.

When you have your own worded summary, become familiar with Scripture that expounds on each key point. And when I say "familiar," I mean know the passage, know the context, and speak the words (at least an accurate paraphrase) without having to even open a Bible. This will take some time, but, remember, there is nothing more important than the gospel message, and no better way to love someone than to share the gospel with them.

Sharing the Gospel

For instance, here is what I would use:

1. God created us in his image and for his own desires (Gen 1:26–17; Job 33:4; Heb 2:5–8).
2. Our sinful nature has separated us from God (Gen 3; Eccl 7:20; Rom 3:9–20, 23).
3. God's son, Jesus Christ, being both fully God as well as fully man, lived the perfect life and became the final sacrifice for sins (John 14:6, 2 Cor 5:21; Phil 5:2–8; Heb 4:14–16).
4. Those (and only those) who repent, confessing faith in Jesus as their savior are 1) reconciled with God, and 2) filled with the Holy Spirit for guidance (John 14:6; Rom 5:1–2; 8:26; 10:9).

Romans Road

One common way of learning how to evangelize and share the gospel message is called Romans Road to Salvation, or more often, Romans Road. This is a simple, memorable, and popular way to summarize the gospel. I'm not necessarily advocating for it, but I'm certainly not advocating against it. The pros are that it may be easier to recall and, more importantly, it's biblical. The con is that the effort of studying Scripture and pulling from the Old Testament, the Gospels, and other epistles (as well as Revelation) may be more worth your time, leading to a deeper understanding of Scripture.

Romans Road focuses on five scriptures from the book of Romans:

- 3:23 –We are all sinners.
- 6:23—The wages of sin is death.
- 5:8—God enacted his plan of salvation as an expression of his love for us.
- 10:9-10—We must confess Jesus as Lord.
- 10:13—Salvation through Jesus is assured.

Again, this may be a great way for you to learn the most imperative points of the gospel message. I would encourage you to continue on once you've learned it, though. Don't rest in the knowledge of five Bible verses, but push yourself to connect similar concepts through all of Scripture, recognizing the complexity, compassion, and endurance of God's plan for salvation.

Remember, there is no message you have that is more important than the gospel. Dave Furman is a remarkable pastor of a church in Dubai. Part of his life story is that he developed severe nerve pain in his arms, which has left him with very minimal use of them. He wrote a book called *Being There* to encourage Christians on "how to love those who are hurting." His book is drenched in the gospel message. Furman explains, "Whether your life seems pain-free or pain-full, you should never get over the gospel. Suffering people are inundated with good advice all the time. Sometimes they even hear good reports from doctors or others. But somebody needs to bring them good news. This is the heart of a Christian's ministry—it's the sharing of good news for the benefit of not only non-Christians but also Christians."[4] Even those who find themselves in overwhelming pain, grief, or any kind of suffering still need the gospel message more than anything else. Of course, we should not neglect caring for physical and here-and-now needs when we are able to do so, but that still does not subvert their need for the gospel.

We are all dying men and women, as we discussed in chapter 4. Some folks may live long lives, pain free through most of it. Others may suffer through cancer, ALS, or Alzheimer's. Yet others may have their lives cut short from a freak car accident or something crazy like a terrorist attack. No matter one's life expectancy, the gospel is the most important news for them to hear, and sharing it with them is your most important responsibility to them.

What Is Your Story?

Hopefully one day you will be put on the spot and need to explain why you are a Christian. Honestly, if you never see that day, you may want to question how much importance you have placed on sharing your faith. First Peter 3:15 says, "But in your hearts honor Christ the Lord as holy, *always being prepared to make a defense to anyone who asks you for a reason for the hope that is in you*; yet do it with gentleness and respect" (emphasis added).

Peter instructs us to *always* be prepared to defend our faith. Always. It's generally easy to talk about why you are a Christian when a youth pastor gives you a week or two to prepare something. I would say it's also generally easy to do so when you are on a mission trip. After all, on a mission trip, you are in Appalachia, the inner city, Mexico, Haiti, or Africa because you

---

4. Furman, *Being There*, 65.

Sharing the Gospel

are acting out your faith. You may expect or even look forward to telling someone about Jesus. But how about the person who asks you why you're praying before lunch when you only have ten minutes until you need to be in class? Or maybe you just got a text from your boyfriend breaking up with you, but someone asks about the Bible you're carrying. How about someone who just rear-ended you and while sharing insurance information he asks about your church bumper sticker? *Always* be prepared to give a defense, regardless of the circumstances or your mood.

In order to work out your defense, ask yourself some questions:

- What is a Christian?
- Why am I a Christian?
- When did I become a Christian?
- Where was I when I became a Christian?
- Who led me to Christ?
- How did I become a Christian?
- How does someone else become a Christian?

There are plenty other questions you should ask yourself, but this is a good start. These are the types of questions you want to ask yourself before someone else asks you. Remember, there is no message you have that is more important than the gospel message. Also keep in mind that the pastor you listen to every week, or the blogger you're always reading—he or she does not have a better gospel message than you. The good news Billy Graham proclaimed to sold-out arenas is the same good news you have. The life, death, and resurrection of Jesus Christ is the news everyone needs to hear, and, Christian, it's your responsibility to help spread it.

Conclusion

We have walked through three common issues facing young Christians:

1. Youth is no obstacle to Christ.
2. The world is an enemy of God.
3. Respond by loving God and loving others.

This isn't a perfect plan of how to engage the world as a young Christian, but it's a good start.

The challenges young adults face now and in the years ahead are vast. Going away to college is to step deep into the mire of secularism. The United States is moving further and further away from whatever civil religion existed for centuries, often leaving Christians as outsiders and exiles in the land they live. Former sexual taboos such as fornication and pornography are now celebrated and common.

Here's the thing, though: you have more opportunities to share the gospel than many generations of Americans before you. If less people are familiar with God's Word, there are more people to reach. While social media and other forms of communication may reveal the ugly side of humanity, they also provide the opportunity to shine a light in the darkness to masses. Consider what God is doing in a place like China, where the Christian faith is spreading like a wildfire, even while the government does all it can to stamp it out. The darker the world is, the brighter Christ shines.

Yes, you have hurdles placed in front of you as a young Christian. Many of these obstacles your parents, pastors, and professors never dealt with at your age. And yes, the world is an enemy of God, but it has been an enemy of God ever since Adam and Eve took those first bites of forbidden fruit. Jesus told his disciples, "The harvest is plentiful, but the laborers are

Conclusion

few. Therefore pray earnestly to the Lord of the harvest to send out laborers into his harvest" (Luke 10:2). You are one of the laborers. Think about that. When Jesus spoke these words, he had *you* in mind. Jesus instructed his disciples to pray for *you*. This verse has been read by Christians for over 2,000 years, leading many of them to pray for . . . *you*.

There is work to be done, young Christian. The best advice I can give is to serve Christ above all. It's not an easy life, but it's a life worth living.

Bibliography

Alliance Defending Freedom. "Elane Photography v. Willock." April 7, 2014. http://www.adfmedia.org/news/prdetail/5537.

Arnett, Jeffrey Jensen. "Emerging Adulthood: A Theory of Development from the Late Teens through the Twenties." *American Psychologist* 55 (2000) 469–80.

Babylon Bee. "32-Year-Old Forcibly Transferred From College Ministry to Singles' Ministry." *Babylon Bee*, May 6, 2016. https://babylonbee.com/news/32-year-old-forcibly-transferred-college-ministry-singles-ministry/.

Baker, Hunter. *The End of Secularism*. Wheaton, IL: Crossway, 2009.

———, interview guest. "Hunter Baker on Secularism," *Research on Religion* (podcast), May 28, 2012. http://www.researchonreligion.org/christianity/hunter-baker-on-secularism.

Baldwin, Michael. "NFL Kickers' Careers Can Last Much Longer than Average Players." *The Oklahoman*, September 3, 2012. http://newsok.com/article/3706375.

Barna Group. "A Snapshot of Faith Practices Across Age Groups." July 23, 2019. https://www.barna.com/research/faithview-on-faith-practice/

Baucham, Voddie. *Family Shepherds: Calling and Equipping Men to Lead Their Homes*. Wheaton, IL: Crossway, 2001.

Beinzee. "A Gift of a Bible." YouTube video, July 8, 2010. https://www.youtube.com/watch?v=6md638smQd8&t=245s.

Bible Hub. "Dioko." https://biblehub.com/greek/1377.htm.

Blackwell, Tom. "Ban Conscientious Objection by Canadian Doctors, Urge Ethicists in Volatile Commentary." *National Post*, September 22, 2016. http://nationalpost.com/health/ban-conscientious-objection-by-canadian-doctors-urge-ethicists-in-volatile-commentary?__lsa=4d00-074e/.

Bruce, F. F. *The Message of the New Testament*. Grand Rapids: Eerdmans, 1972.

Bureau of Democracy, Human Rights and Labor. *International Religious Freedom Report for 2015: Executive Summary*. U.S. Department of State, 2015. https://2009-2017.state.gov/j/drl/rls/irf/religiousfreedom/index.htm#wrapper.

Carnevale, Anthony P., et al. *Recovery: Job Growth and Education Requirements Through 2020: Executive Summary*. https://cew.georgetown.edu/wp-content/uploads/2014/11/Recovery2020.ES_.Web_.pdf.

Carney, Matthew. "Chinese Communist Party Readies Crackdown on Christianity." *Australian Broadcasting Company*, October 7, 2016. http://www.abc.net.au/news/2016-10-08/chinese-communist-partys-crackdown-on-religion/7912140.

Bibliography

Carter, Joe. "The FAQs: Persecution of Christians in Iraq." *The Gospel Coalition*, July 25, 2015. https://www.thegospelcoalition.org/article/the-faqs-persecution-of-christians-in-iraq/

———. "9 Things You Should Know About Islamic State." *The Gospel Coalition*, November 14, 2015. https://www.thegospelcoalition.org/article/9-things-you-should-know-about-islamic-state/.

Castillo, Michelle. "Millennials are the Most Stressed Generation, Survey Finds." *CBS News*, February 11, 2013. https://www.cbsnews.com/news/millennials-are-the-most-stressed-generation-survey-finds/.

Challies, Tim. "7 Marks of a False Teacher." June 20, 2013. https://www.challies.com/articles/7-marks-of-a-false-teacher/?utm_content=buffer56219&utm_medium=social&utm_source=facebook.com&utm_campaign=buffer.

Chan, Francis, and Lisa Chan. *You and Me Forever*. San Francisco: Clair Love, 2014.

Chandler, Adam. "What Is an Islamic Caliphate and Why Did ISIS Make One?" *The Atlantic*, June 30, 2014. https://www.theatlantic.com/international/archive/2014/06/what-is-an-islamic-caliphate-and-why-did-isis-make-one/373693/.

"ISIS Video Appears to Show Beheadings of Egyptian Coptic Christians in Libya." *CNN*, February 16, 2015. http://www.cnn.com/2015/02/15/middleeast/isis-video-beheadings-christians/.

College Board. "Trends in College Pricing." https://trends.collegeboard.org/college-pricing/figures-tables/tuition-fees-room-and-board-over-time.

Dever, Mark. *Discipling: How to Help Others Follow Jesus*. Wheaton, IL: Crossway, 2016.

DeYoung, Kevin. *The Hole in Our Holiness: Filling the Gap between Gospel Passion and the Pursuit of Godliness*. Wheaton, IL: Crossway, 2012.

———, *Taking God at His Word: Why the Bible Is Knowable, Necessary, and Enough, and What that Means for You and Me*. Wheaton, IL: Crossway, 2014.

Dimock, Michael. "Defining Generations: Where Millennials End and Generation Z Begins." Pew Research Center, January 19, 2019. https://www.pewresearch.org/fact-tank/2019/01/17/where-millennials-end-and-generation-z-begins/.

Dreher, Rod. "Rainbow Cake Girl: The True Story." *The American Conservative*, January 17, 2020. https://www.theamericanconservative.com/dreher/the-rainbow-cake-girl-what-the-media-are-hiding/.

Dunn, Richard R., Jana L. Sundene. *Shaping the Journey of Emerging Adults: Life-Giving Rhythms for Spiritual Transformation*. Downers Grove, IL: InterVarsity, 2012.

Fam, Mariam, and Hamza Hendawi. "Bomb Kills 25 at Egypt's Main Coptic Christian Cathedral." *AP News*, December 11, 2016. https://apnews.com/ofdc6cfod7424cf7aac64ed6df982208?utm_campaign=SocialFlow&utm_source=Twitter&utm_medium=AP.

Ferguson, Everett. "Persecution in the Early Church: Did You Know?" *Christianity Today* 9/3 (issue 27, 1990). https://www.christianitytoday.com/history/issues/issue-27/persecution-in-early-church-did-you-know.html.

Foxe, John. *Foxe's Book of Martyrs*. Edited by and William Byron Forbush. http://kotisatama.net/files/kotisatama/Tekstit_ja_kirjat/foxe.pdf.

French, David. "In *Masterpiece Cakeshop*, Justice Kennedy Strikes a Blow for the Dignity of the Faithful." *National Review*, June 4, 2018. https://www.nationalreview.com/2018/06/masterpiece-cakeshop-ruling-religious-liberty-victory/.

Bibliography

Friedersdorf, Conor. "Refusing to Photograph a Gay Wedding Isn't Hateful." *The Atlantic*, March 5, 2014. https://www.theatlantic.com/politics/archive/2014/03/refusing-to-photograph-a-gay-wedding-isnt-hateful/284224/.

Furman, Dave. *Being There: How to Love Those Who Are Hurting*. Wheaton, IL: Crossway, 2016.

Gilbert, Greg. "What Is the Gospel?" Crossway, October 7, 2016. https://www.crossway.org/articles/what-is-the-gospel-2/.

Greenslade, Roy. "Iran Jails Women Journalists." *The Guardian*, September 11, 2012. https://www.theguardian.com/media/greenslade/2012/sep/11/press-freedom-iran.

Hannigan, Dave. "Religious Class Leaves USA'S Best Left Back an Observer of World Cup Bid." *The Irish Times*, June 12, 2019. https://www.irishtimes.com/sport/soccer/international/religious-clash-leaves-usa-s-best-left-back-an-observer-of-world-cup-bid-1.3923456.

Hill, Jonathan P. *Emerging Adulthood and Faith*. Grand Rapids: Calvin College Press, 2015.

Hinn, Benny. *The Anointing*. Nashville: T. Nelson, 1992.

Hoffower, Hillary. "Depression Is on the Rise among Gen Z—And Teen Girls Are Experiencing the Worst of it." *Business Insider*, July 14, 2019. https://www.businessinsider.com/depression-increasing-among-teens-gen-z-2019-7.

Hong, Brendon. "China's Crackdown on Christian Churches." *Daily Beast*, May 8, 2016. https://www.thedailybeast.com/chinas-crackdown-on-christian-churches.

Horton, Michael. "Evangelicals Should Be Deeply Troubled by Donald Trump's Attempt to Mainstream Heresy." *The Washington Post*, January 3, 2017. https://www.washingtonpost.com/news/acts-of-faith/wp/2017/01/03/evangelicals-should-be-deeply-troubled-by-donald-trumps-attempt-to-mainstream-heresy/.

Howard, Jacqueline. "Increasing Social Media Use Tied to Rise in Teens' Depression Symptoms, Study Says." *CNN*, July 15, 2019. https://www.cnn.com/2019/07/15/health/social-media-depression-teens-study/index.html.

Idleman, Kyle. *Not a Fan: Becoming a Completely Committed Follower of Jesus*. Grand Rapids,: Zondervan, 2011.

Inazu, John. "Democrats Are Going to Regret Beto's Stance on Conservative Churches." *The Atlantic*, October 12, 2019. https://www.theatlantic.com/ideas/archive/2019/10/beto-orourkes-pluralism-failure/599953/?fbclid=IwAR0Sv5U3UR_SfimHxVxpIH4g7yo7x-YZqqOj2vfIOAYwV1g6gA7BBvUr1kE.

Johnson, Ian. "Decapitated Churches on China's Christian Heartland. *The New York Times*, May 21, 2016. https://www.nytimes.com/2016/05/22/world/asia/china-christians-zhejiang.html.

Jones, Mark. "What Is a Covenant?" Ligonier Ministries, May 1, 2014. https://www.ligonier.org/learn/articles/what-covenant/.

Kellogg, Amy. "Iran Sentences American Pastor Saeed Abedini to 8 Years in Prison." *Fox News*, January 27, 2013. http://www.foxnews.com/world/2013/01/27/iran-sentences-american-pastor-saeed-abedini-to-8-years-in-prison.html.

Kidd, Thomas. "China Sentences Pastor Wang Yi to Nine Years in Prison." *The Gospel Coalition*, December 30, 2019. https://www.thegospelcoalition.org/blogs/evangelical-history/china-sentences-pastor-wang-yi-nine-years-prison/.

Kinnaman, David, and Mark Matlock. *Faith for Exiles: 5 Ways for a New Generation to Follow Jesus in Digital Babylon*. Grand Rapids: Baker, 2019.

Bibliography

Kuo, Lily. "In China, They're Closing Churches, Jailing Pastors—And Even Rewriting Scripture." *The Guardian*, January 13, 2019. https://www.theguardian.com/world/2019/jan/13/china-christians-religious-persecution-translation-bible.
Kurth, James. "Western Civilization, Our Tradition." *The Intercollegiate Review*, Fall 2003/Spring 2004, 5-13.
Lewis, C. S. *Mere Christianity*. San Francisco: HarperOne, 1952.
Machen, J. Gresham. *Christianity and Liberalism*. Grand Rapids: Eerdmans, 1923.
Martin, Asia. "What's the Return on a College Education?" *Forbes*, August 22, 2019. https://www.forbes.com/advisor/personal-finance/whats-the-return-on-a-college-education/?tid=social&utm_source=FBPAGE&utm_medium=social&utm_content=3002832479&utm_campaign=sprinklrForbesMainFB.
McCauley, Kim. "What on Earth Is U.S. Soccer Doing with Jaeline Hinkle?" *SBNation*, July 25, 2018. https://www.sbnation.com/soccer/2018/7/25/17609060/jaelene-hinkle-uswnt-roster-tournament-of-nations-roster-homophobic-700-club-interview.
McCracken, Brett. "*Righteous Gemstones* and Hollywood's Christian Villains." *The Gospel Coalition*, August 31, 2019. https://www.thegospelcoalition.org/article/righteous-gemstones-and-hollywoods-christian-villains/.
McLaughlin, Eliott C. "ISIS Executes More Christians in Libya, Video Shows." *CNN*, April 20, 2015. http://www.cnn.com/2015/04/19/africa/libya-isis-executions-ethiopian-christians/
Merida, Tony. *Exalting Jesus in 1 & 2 Timothy and Titus (Christ-Centered Exposition)*. Nashville: B&H, 2013.
Miller, Eric. "Daniel: Numbered, Weighed...Divided?" from Bloomsburg Christian Church, Bloomsburg, PA. May 22, 2016. https://vimeo.com/168977672
Mohler, Albert. *The Briefing* (podcast), episode aired September 28, 2016. https://albertmohler.com/2016/09/28/briefing-09-28-16/.
Moore, Russell. *Onward: Engaging the Culture Without Losing the Gospel*. Nashville: B&H, 2015.
———. "You Only Live Forever." November 3, 2015. https://www.russellmoore.com/2015/11/03/you-only-live-forever/.
Morello, Carol. "State Department Criticizes Blasphemy Laws in Muslim Nations." *The Washington Post*, August 10, 2016. https://www.washingtonpost.com/world/national-security/state-department-criticizes-blasphemy-laws-in-muslim-nations/2016/08/10/48f16242-5f11-11e6-af8e-54aa2e849447_story.html?utm_term=.0da32ca8c08a.
Nardi, William Z. "Xi Jinping Ramps Up Religious Persecution." *National Review*, July 29, 2019. https://www.nationalreview.com/2019/07/religious-persecution-china-xi-jinping/.
Osteen, Joel. *Your Best Life Now: 7 Steps to Living at Your Full Potential*. New York: FaithWords, 2004.
Packer, J. I. *Concise Theology*. Carol Stream, IL: Tyndale, 1993.
Perry, Jackie Hill. *Gay Girl, Good God*. Nashville: B&H, 2018.
"Persecute." *Merriam-Webster*. https://www.merriam-webster.com/dictionary/persecute.
Piper, John. "As We Forgive Our Debtors: What Does Forgiveness Look Like?" *Desiring God* (website), March 20, 1994. https://www.desiringgod.org/messages/as-we-forgive-our-debtors.

Bibliography

———. "How Much Authority Does Satan Have in the World?" *Ask Pastor John* (podcast), May 28, 2019. https://www.desiringgod.org/interviews/how-much-authority-does-satan-have-in-the-world.

———. "May I Split My Giving Between My Church and Another Ministry?" *Ask Pastor John* (podcast), February 16, 2016. https://www.desiringgod.org/interviews/may-i-split-my-giving-between-my-church-and-another-ministry.

Platt, David. *Counter Culture: A Compassionate Call to Counter Culture in a World of Poverty, Same-Sex Marriage, Racism, Sex Slavery, Immigration, Abortion, Persecution, Orphans, and Pornography.* Carol Stream, IL: Tyndale, 2015.

Pope, Charles. "The Five Stages of Religious Persecution." September 1, 2014. http://blog.adw.org/2014/09/the-five-stages-of-religious-persecution/.

Pruitt, Shane. *9 Common Lies Christians Believe: And Why God's Truth is Infinitely Better.* New York: Multomah, 2019.

———. "7 Common Traits of Gen Z: In Their Own Words." September 5, 2019. http://www.shanepruitt.com/7-common-traits-of-gen-z-in-their-own-words/?fbclid=IwAR1q27RchEIJsykD6s2xlSkH9SsJ-w7GroJuSOxM24M7xDcnJSzp2UDY1dk.

Rampell, Catherine. "The College Degree Has Become the New High School Degree." *The Washington Post*, September 9, 2014. https://www.washingtonpost.com/opinions/catherine-rampell-the-college-degree-has-become-the-new-high-school-degree/2014/09/08/e935b68c-378a-11e4-8601-97ba88884ffd_story.html.

Reitz, Erica Young. *After College: Navigating Transitions, Relationships and Faith.* Downers Grove, IL: InterVarsity, 2016.

Root, Kayla, and Ben Gill. "This Pro Soccer Player Gave Up the US Women's Team Just So She Could Stand for Her Faith." *CBN News*, June 1, 2018. https://www1.cbn.com/cbnnews/entertainment/2018/june/this-pro-soccer-player-gave-up-the-us-womens-team-just-so-she-could-stand-for-her-faith.

Sekulow, Jordan. "American Pastor Andrew Brunson Wrongfully Prisoned in Turkey." American Center for Law and Justice, 2016. https://aclj.org/persecuted-church/american-pastor-andrew-brunson-wrongfully-imprisoned-in-turkey.

Sherwood, Harriet. "Asia Bibi Begins New Life in Canada—But Her Ordeal May Not Be Over." *The Guardian*, May 8, 2019. https://www.theguardian.com/world/2019/may/08/asia-bibi-begins-new-life-in-canada-but-her-ordeal-may-not-be-over.

Skeldon, Grant. *The Passion Generation: The Seemingly Reckless, Definitely Disruptive, but Far from Hopeless Millennials.* Grand Rapids: Zondervan, 2018.

Smith, Christian, et al. *Lost in Transition: The Dark Side of Emerging Adulthood.* New York: Oxford University Press, 2011.

"Soccer Player Hears Boos over Her Past LGBTQ Protest." *The New York Post*, May 31, 2018. https://nypost.com/2018/05/31/soccer-player-hears-boos-over-her-past-lgbtq-protest/.

Sproul, R. C. "What Does the Word 'Gospel' Mean in the New Testament?" Ligonier Ministries, May 25, 2016. https://www.ligonier.org/blog/what-does-word-gospel-mean-new-testament/.

———. "What Is the Gospel?" Ligonier Ministries, February 7, 2018. https://www.ligonier.org/blog/what-is-the-gospel/.

Stuart, Chase. "A Closer Look at Running Back Age Patterns." *Football Perspective*, July 2, 2012. http://www.footballperspective.com/a-closer-look-at-running-back-aging-patterns/.

Tozer, A. W. *The Pursuit of God.* Chicago: Moody, 1948.

Bibliography

U.S. Bureau of Labor Statistics. "Labor Force Statistics from the Current Population Survey." https://data.bls.gov/timeseries/LNS14000000.

Vanderstelt, Jeff. *Gospel Fluency: Speaking the Truths of Jesus into the Everyday Stuff of Life*. Wheaton, IL: Crossway, 2017.

Voice of the Martyrs. "About VOM." https://www.persecution.com/about/.

———. "Prisoner Profile: Asia Bibi." https://www.prisoneralert.com/pprofiles/vp_prisoner_197_profile.html.

———. *2017 Global Report on Where Christians are Persecuted Today*. 2017. https://vom.com.au/wp-content/uploads/2017/05/Global-Report-2017_au.pdf.

———. *2019 Global Prayer Guide*. 2019. https://vom.com.au/wp-content/uploads/2019/06/2019-Global-Prayer-Guide.pdf.

Washer, Paul. "Christ, the True Vine: John 15." HeartCry Missionary Society, 2013. https://vimeo.com/42767259.

Yancey, George. "Is There Really Anti-Christian Discrimination in America?" *The Gospel Coalition*, August 19, 2019. https://www.thegospelcoalition.org/article/anti-christian-discrimination-america/.

———. "What Is Persecution?" *Patheos*, May 28, 2019. https://www.patheos.com/blogs/shatteringparadigms/2019/05/1928/.

Yeghnazar, David. "5 Ways Persecution in Iran Has Backfired." *The Gospel Coalition*, October 11, 2016. https://www.thegospelcoalition.org/article/5-ways-persecution-in-iran-has-backfired/.

"Youth." *Dictionary.com*. https://www.dictionary.com/browse/youth?s=t.

Zaimov, Stoyan. "Church Leader's Wife Buried Alive by Chinese Authorities for Protesting Church Demolition." *The Christian Post*, April 19, 2016. https://www.christianpost.com/news/china-church-leaders-wife-buried-alive-killed-for-protesting-church-demolition-162067/.

———. "Hundreds of Police in China Demolish Church Crosses, Leave Christian Protesters Beaten and Bloodied." *The Christian Post*, March 31, 2016. https://www.christianpost.com/news/china-police-demolish-church-crosses-christian-protesters-beaten-bloodied-160583/.

———. "Iran's House Church Movement Witnessing 'Astounding' Growth; Hundreds Being Baptized." *The Christian Post*, November 16, 2016. https://www.christianpost.com/news/irans-house-church-movement-witnessing-astounding-growth-hundreds-being-baptized-171526/.

www.ingramcontent.com/pod-product-compliance
Lightning Source LLC
Chambersburg PA
CBHW070913160426
43193CB00011B/1445